PENGUIN BOOKS

RETHINK AGEING

Reshmi Chakraborty is the co-founder and Editor of Silver Talkies, a social enterprise focused on active ageing since 2014. She has worked as a journalist for over two decades and continues to write for various publications. She believes in highlighting skill and initiative in older adults, many of whom are discovering new avenues at a later age. Reshmi loves to travel, attempts to read everything she can find and is trying in vain to get over her Netflix and Twitter addiction. This is her first book.

Nidhi Chawla is the co-founder and Business & Strategy Head of Silver Talkies. She has several years of experience in the financial services sector, having worked with SREI International Securities as well as McKinsey & Company. Nidhi has received several leadership awards for her work in the eldercare space and is currently a member of the CII Seniorcare committee. When she isn't busy dreaming about the next big idea for enriching the lives of seniors, you will find her working out or flipping through three different books that are always on her table. This is her first book.

Silver Talkies is a pioneering social enterprise on a mission since 2014 to make healthy and active ageing a desirable and viable goal for older adults. Their belief is that active ageing is the most promising and economical form of preventive healthcare and with an empowering and enabling environment, older adults can age gracefully and with dignity.

Visit them on www.silvertalkies.com to know more.

ADVANCE PRAISE FOR THE BOOK

'Getting older doesn't have to mean your life stops! *Rethink Ageing* brilliantly explores finding new meaning, passion and excitement in older age.'

—Dr Marshall Goldsmith, Thinkers50 #1 Executive Coach
and *New York Times* bestselling author of *The Earned Life*,
Triggers, and *What Got You Here Won't Get You There*

'It is heartening that a book on ageing is being written which does not treat it as an affliction or disability. There is much that one can do irrespective of age and among those things is work to help improve one's immediate surroundings and provide such help as one is qualified to give. More importantly, one can lead a full life meeting people in different groups—literary groups or bridge, chess or other groups. Not of the old, but of those who share the same interests.

My warmest congratulations to those who thought of this book. I'm sure it will be of interest to all those interested in the subjects covered and not just in old people.'

—Bhaskar Ghose, IAS (Retd), former Secretary to the
Government of India, Ministry of Information &
Broadcasting and Ministry of Culture

'As someone who has always embraced change with enthusiasm (much like my mother), I feel vindicated that finally, the discussion around growing old has opened up. Fear and ignorance is being replaced by curiosity and possibilities. This book goes a long way in helping that process along—it puts the spotlight on the issues we try to ignore, from sex to senility and in doing so, helps us all—old and young—to discover the potential of the "sunset" years. I'm surprised to find that my life has become so much more interesting to me as I've aged, and I hope many more will be thus surprised!'

—Ratna Pathak Shah, Actor

'Ageing is commonly associated with disease and episodes of medical care. However, Reshmi and Nidhi have offered helpful advice through *Rethink Ageing* to ease into active and healthy ageing. Interspersed with inspiring stories and pragmatic possibilities, the book is a handy guide peeking into the future of elderly care.'

—Dr Devi Shetty, Founder and Chairman,
Senior Cardiac Surgeon, Narayana Health

RETHINK AGEING

LESSONS IN AGEING FROM THE OLDER AND BOLDER GENERATION

Reshmi Chakraborty
Nidhi Chawla

PENGUIN BOOKS

An imprint of Penguin Random House

PENGUIN BOOKS

USA | Canada | UK | Ireland | Australia
New Zealand | India | South Africa | China

Penguin Books is part of the Penguin Random House group of companies
whose addresses can be found at global.penguinrandomhouse.com

Published by Penguin Random House India Pvt. Ltd
4th Floor, Capital Tower 1, MG Road,
Gurugram 122 002, Haryana, India

First published in Penguin Books by Penguin Random House India 2022

Copyright © Reshmi Chakraborty and Nidhi Chawla 2022

All rights reserved

10 9 8 7 6 5 4 3 2 1

The views and opinions expressed in this book are the authors' own and the
facts are as reported by them which have been verified to the extent possible,
and the publishers are not in any way liable for the same.

ISBN 9780143453666

Typeset in Adobe Caslon Pro by Manipal Technologies Limited, Manipal

www.penguin.co.in

For
Ma, Baba, Mummy, Papa
—Reshmi

For
Biji, Mummy, Papa, Appa, Amma
—Nidhi

And to all the elders of Silver Talkies community and beyond

Contents

Introduction

Getting old is like climbing a mountain; you get a little out of breath, but the view is much better!

Ingrid Bergman

Ageing: The Multiple-Lens View

Rio Olympics 2016. Usain Bolt, the fastest man on earth, is getting ready for his 100m dash. Bolt stands a chance to create history if he wins his third Olympic gold this time. Among the cluster of photographers waiting to catch that moment is Seshadri Sukumar, a Chennai shutterbug. Sukumar had never quite imagined himself waiting in one spot for four-and-a-half hours as a witness to one of the greatest sporting moments in history. But over the years, he has done just that. From the time he stepped into his late fifties and sixties, Sukumar has covered several Olympic Games, FIFA World Cups, Asian Games and every major cricket tournament India has played. A photograph taken by him graces the cover of Sachin Tendulkar's autobiography.

At sixty-six, Sukumar is living a life he hadn't even dreamt of in his early years, as he lugs around cameras and lenses weighing over 20 kilos, swiftly moving from the Tokyo Olympics to the ICC T20 World Cup 2021. Age is never on his mind. 'I'm energized by a good photograph and the process of it', he says. 'And I'm just getting started!'

If you ask Sukumar whether this is how he thought life would work out in his sixties, the answer would be a big no. From a conventional lens, it's hard to imagine a genial-looking former bank official globetrotting behind sports superstars, in his sixties. Yet, given the times of late-life transitions we are living in, it's equally easy to visualize that and not surprising at all.

Least of all to us. Being part of Silver Talkies, our social impact organization, in the last seven years has been our biggest lesson and has taught us to rethink every stereotype associated with age, ever. We have seen older adults transition to jobs, hobbies, lives and loves they have always dreamt of or discovered despite having never imagined before, often in their so-called 'twilight years,' a term that's one of the biggest misnomers ever.

The World Health Organization (WHO) would call older adults like Sukumar active agers. If you read about ageing or have an interest in the area, you've probably heard the term *active ageing* as it has made its way into conversations about age in urban India. But what is active and healthy ageing? WHO describes it as the process of developing and maintaining functional abilities that enable well-being in later years. This means regardless of gender, socio-economic status, disability and health, a person growing older should have the chance to live life fully engaged and to their best ability, across various well-being markers—physical, social, emotional, vocational, cognitive and spiritual. Simply put, age shouldn't be the hurdle you need to jump over to live the life you want.

Active ageing is the way growing older is being redefined across India and the world, even though the mindset change is sometimes a slow one.

When we started Silver Talkies, it was with a desire to bring together opportunities of engagement for every urban older adult whose lives we could touch. It was also a chance to tell the stories of people who chose never to let the years get in their way.

Our ideas and inspirations came from home and beyond as we saw first-hand the transitions our parents experienced in midlife and their sometimes-unintended impact. One of our parents had a home-based venture that she started when her life as a homemaker began changing to leave her with more downtime, with children moving away and her husband no longer in an active nine-to-five job. Another of our parents was an artist at heart, who had let work, family and responsibilities close the door on what had once been a passion for him. When he retired, his daughter, who had witnessed this passion take a back seat over the years, gifted him the best art supplies she could find, in the hope that he fills his retirement years with colours.

But what we wished for and what happened were two different stories.

One of our parents had always been an outdoor person, with an active social life and busy career. We saw that precariously diminishing, as age, retirement and ailments took over. We saw boredom, uncertainty about loss of purpose and lack of opportunities for all our parents despite the drive and skill they had. We tried to look for options to keep our parents engaged and often came back empty-handed.

What we saw at home, translated outside too. We realized there was no single way in which ageing panned out. Some welcomed it and ran with it. Some let it cocoon them in a space of silent acceptance. Some tried to balance an ever-active young mind with an ageing body.

Ageing is an inevitability in all our lives. Yet, the talk around it has often been unidimensional in India, looking at it from the sole viewpoint of health. We prepare extensively for college and first jobs, among life's biggest changes, but there is no preparation ever for midlife and the years after it—one of the other big transition phases. Of course, we talk about retirement and celebrate it. In fact, most Indian family albums are likely to have that one photograph of a parent awarded a watch and a commemoration plaque on D-Day as colleagues clap on. But do we talk about possibilities in the years beyond retirement? Do we pause to think how this transition would go for them and how we can enable them to navigate it better?

Instead, we start instant ageism—asking parents, uncles and aunts to rest up after years of work, to slow down. We've sometimes been similarly overprotective with our own parents. Nidhi's mother sits on the floor to do her daily prayers. Concerned that her mother may find it difficult, Nidhi would often discourage her to do that. Her mother responded that even if sometimes difficult, she wanted to continue the practice until she was able to. It also helped her feel flexible and able. Reshmi often stops herself from pushing her mother to get additional help around the house. 'I know how much I can stretch so don't stop me', her mother says. 'Else I'll start feeling older and inactive sooner.'

What if how older adults wish to live is the opposite of what we conventionally think? What if they are just starting to discover possibilities and raring to go? An interesting survey called Jug Jug Jiyenge done in 2018 by IVH Seniorcare identified a big mismatch between elderly parents' real concerns versus what their children thought concerned them. While 67 per cent of children were worried about their parents' health, the parents themselves—36 per cent of them—were worried about maintaining their social life. 30 per cent of them were worried about managing their daily needs. Only 10 per cent were worried about their health![1]

When we started our social enterprise Silver Talkies in 2014, it was inspired by the idea to discover opportunities and support systems which encouraged older adults who wished to remain active. Yes, there were several upcoming start-ups focusing on the health care aspect of age. But few were looking at the social engagement and empowerment side of it that came from forming new connections and exploring new avenues.

Seven years down the line, we have seen the conversation around ageing start becoming multidimensional around us, and we are proud to have been at the frontline of it. Our first event for older adults wasn't a health or a spiritual talk—the most common options available at that time for senior citizens. It was a visit to an art gallery where a motley bunch of seniors shared coffee and their memories of the Bengaluru of yore with gallery owner Paul Fernandes, himself a senior and acclaimed for his artwork tinged with nostalgia and humour.

We have held a flea market for senior entrepreneurs, giving them an exclusive spotlight to showcase their skills. An Elders' Theatre workshop has given our community members a chance to explore their inner child and find the freedom of expression. We now do events and workshops exclusively for older adults, run a digital magazine and a virtual club that has members who are fifty-five and above, from across India and the world. We conduct classes and workshops that range from language learning to technology, artwork, dance, to name a few. We have had countless talks and workshops on health, too—it being one of the most important aspects of growing older. The reason we list all these down here is not to showcase our work but to emphasize the need to go beyond the linear narrative in the story of growing older. Because an increasing number of older adults in India are doing just that. And breaking down every generational barrier in the process.

Take Sukumar for instance. He was into photography from a very early age. But never did he imagine that in his fifties, he would make a transition that would not just keep him energized for years to come but also give him a sense of purpose and fulfilment.

It's a similar story with many older adults we have met.

Three years ago, Shakuntala Pai walked the ramp in a specially curated fashion show for senior citizens. She wore an off-shoulder dress and sashayed down the catwalk with the confidence of a seasoned model, to loud applause and whistles from the audience, including much of her adoring family. Pai says growing older has given her that confidence and brought her into her own. She has discovered a knack for art in her seventies. A former teacher, Pai was a caregiver to various super seniors in her family for twenty-five years, a common story for many Indian women.

'I feel I finally have free time. I am also asserting myself more as I grow older', Pai tells us, showing us around the room at home she has converted into an art studio, and a colourful Kerala mural she is working on. When Pai rediscovered her love for art, she didn't hold herself back because of age. Instead, she decided to make the most of the time she now had. She explored YouTube for tutorials, discovered she had a talent for picking things up easily and signed up with various teachers to learn Indian folk-art forms. Pai has had her share of health problems—she had a knee surgery a few years ago and minor health problems but chose not to let that come in the way of living life the way she wanted as she aged, with a healthy dose of art!

A few months back, our friend Suchitra sent us a photograph of a cake with the words 'Congratulations Dr Gopinath' written on it. Her mother Sushila Gopinath had just finished her PhD at seventy-five! That's not all. When we called Dr Gopinath to congratulate her, we discovered that the long road to the PhD, which she started in her mid-sixties, wasn't the only thing that kept her active. She'd been learning bridge (playing twice a week), keeping an eye on stocks in the share market and had signed up to translate a book in Sanskrit on the Shankaracharya.

'This constant learning and exercising my brain for this and that keeps me going', she told us. 'I don't have the time to worry about anything negative.'

Hearing such stories may have surprised us and filled us with awe and admiration ten years ago. The awe is still there. But we aren't surprised anymore.

Yet the reality around us shows we do not always account for these myriad sides of ageing as part of the bigger picture. People still hold a typical image of age in their minds, and very often it is of a grey-haired person bent over a stick. We do know a lot of grey-haired people. Forget bending over a stick, some of them can be found on Instagram dishing out life lessons to their younger followers. Others are restarting a new career in the movies or putting their years of corporate experience to use for social good and still clocking in extra-long workdays. It makes us feel that the image of age we hold as a society needs to change, and how.

Ageing is still approached as an indisposition, but as the 'senior citizens' above show us, it is possible to embrace the advancing years and live your best life.

It is also time to look at ageing as a phase of transition, adaptation and gradual acceptance with many faces to it. Active ageing is a reality; so is loneliness, abandonment and loss of purpose. Marathons are a reality for some, as is a frail and weakening body for some others. Almost every day we come across someone who is celebrating the sense of carefreeness that can sometimes come with the older years. We also meet people who may have one foot in the conventional ways of ageing and retirement but are trying to adapt to a quickly changing world.

It isn't an easy adaptation. We are a society-in-transition. Moving from joint families to nuclear; shifting from the old family home to an apartment or senior living; from the traditional model of dependence on children to independence and empowerment. It comes with challenges that can sometimes be unfathomable, where children expect parents to maintain their own lives, yet be available for their needs. Parents, on the other hand, wish their children to be free of responsibilities but do want the assurance of mental and physical support when needed. Given that both generations come with their own viewpoints and traditionally ageing is 'supposed' to be a time to slow down or avoid certain ways of life, it can sometimes lead to mismatched expectations.

A few months ago, we asked a group of older adults what they anonymously wished to tell the younger generation. The answers were simple, yet telling.

Understand me as you wish to be understood. I try my best to understand you and the changing times but I come with a backlog of conditioning which will maybe take some more time to erase.

You may be busy with your work or family, just find time to talk to me even if it's for a short time. That keeps me going forward happily in my day-to-day routine, and that's the only tonic for my happiness.

I like to take my own decisions regarding matters that concern me. I find excessive advice or interference in my affairs to be irksome.

I don't want to interfere in your personal life but I am all ears if you want to discuss anything with me.

As families, and a society, we need to have empathetic conversations and more open intergenerational dialogues to understand ageing from every angle.

But why are we even talking about this now? What is the buzz around age all about, and why write a full-fledged book on how ageing is being rethought? Because the landscape of ageing itself is changing. The Indian family is being reshaped, medical help is available for age-related ailments more than ever, many middle- and upper-middle-class older adults have better economic solvency now than their parents' generation did and most importantly, there has been a change in the mindset around ageing, with independence and self-empowerment becoming keywords of ageing in today's urban India.

We are aware that this book is limited in its scope given that our understanding of ageing and its facets have largely been in an urban sphere. Even within that sphere there are several angles to ageing, with varying levels of privilege—birth, education and economics being some—that make it a different reality for different people. We may have missed out on capturing many of those realities. Ageing in rural India remains an unexplored territory for us. We hope to have a deeper understanding of these as our horizon and knowledge widens.

The evolving landscape of ageing, reshaping of the family structure in India and the resulting challenges and issues call for giving age, and the possibilities that come with it, a relook from multiple lenses. Because ageing, truly is, what you make of it—a time for exploring, empowering, reinventing or even withdrawing. The choice is yours. The idea behind our work and this book is to emphasize that these choices exist.

We have seen these diverse choices play out before our eyes since we began working with older adults. With stories of ageing, its drawbacks and how to navigate them, acceptance and making the best use of the positives that come with it, we hope this book will help you or an older loved one find a way to age better, healthier and happier.

1

Older & Bolder: Changing Face of Age in India

One cannot live the afternoon of life according to the program of life's morning, for what was great in the morning will be of little importance in the evening and what in the morning was true, at evening will have become a lie.

Carl Jung

Rajini Chandy isn't afraid of anything. At seventy, the homemaker-turned-actress from Kerala is open to challenges and trying anything at least once, no matter what the outcome may be. 'I love myself', says Chandy. 'I want to run, I run. I want to laugh loudly, I laugh loudly.'

Chandy walks the talk. In 2020, when photographer Athira Joy requested her to do a glamourous photo shoot, belying ageist stereotypes, Chandy found the idea interesting and went ahead—breaking the 'traditional grandmother' stereotype, dressed in Western clothes, looking confident, fit and ready to take on the world. The photographs went viral on social media, unleashing a torrent of reactions that included positive comments but also misogynist trolling asking her to spend time in religion or taking care of the family at 'her age'.

The reactions left an emotional scar but didn't stop Chandy from doing what she wanted to do. 'At seventy, I don't know how many more twenty-four hours I have, right? I want to fill it with things that make me happy. I don't want to think I can't do this or that because of age or some aches and pain or what society thinks.'

Chandy is now a common face in several advertisements. Her recently launched YouTube channel's mission is to inspire others not to be limited by their years and push boundaries where they can.

Ageing is seeing a turning point in the urban Indian world. Like Chandy, there are many others who do not feel limited by their years. In fact, some of them welcome it with open arms.

'Never thought I would be so excited to greet the big sixty!' Graduating from junior to senior and gaining the license to get more wild and free!' That's Kanchana Arni, an author and folk-art expert from Bengaluru messaging us after we wished her on her sixtieth birthday. Arni, who has spent the last few years exploring diverse interests and activities given that she is free of certain family responsibilities, feels she's just getting started.

Do you relate to Chandy and Arni's emotion—looking old on the outside but bubbling with the energy and enthusiasm of a young adult on the inside? Meet the new emerging faces of ageing India!

'I don't feel old; I feel I am starting to live my life only now'

These are some common remarks we have heard since we set up Silver Talkies in 2014. We work with older adults to fill the gap of social engagement in their lives and empower them with opportunities and resources. 'You have to grow mentally as you age', says Bina Mirchandani, chief faculty at Rtambhara Wellness Pvt. Ltd. and a senior herself. Mirchandani keeps her days and life full, playing a doting grandmother but over and above engaging in professional and personal pursuits that keep the ingenuity of her mind ongoing. A believer in the 'growth mindset', she believes growth—whether it comes through learning or by being part of a stimulating network—is what keeps one energized and alive.

Over the years we have seen older people get doctorates at seventy-five, learn how to swim after sixty and start a new venture at sixty-five, without being limited by age—aided by emerging opportunities, technology, peer support and an increasing awareness of possibilities. Peer groups and social connections are often the stand-out factors here, and we've seen older adults who had withdrawn or grown quieter due to a life change like spousal bereavement or ailment, gradually break out of their shell supported by encouragement and inspiration from others.

On World Elders' Day on 1 October 2021, a group of members of Silver Talkies Club, run by us for people over fifty-five, presented artworks they had created in a virtual party we had organized. The theme—age is what you let it be for you. Whether sixty or eighty, nowhere was there any sign of life coming to a halt in those artworks. Instead, their creations spoke about the travels they were planning to undertake once the pandemic lifted, the skills they wished to learn and the principles they wished to master. All of them, irrespective of age, had miles to go and they were actively working towards it.

That small virtual art party anecdote is a reflection of the transition many urban older adults are experiencing as they go through life changes brought about by growing older, empty nests and retirement, to name a few. Many of them are becoming more independent-minded and empowered, investing the time and resources they now have at their disposal to age better and rethink their lives to lead the years ahead in a gainful and healthy way. Of course, this rewiring is not universal and often has a strong economic background as a solid base. It's largely happening among middle- to upper-income people, driven by socio-economic factors, nuclear families and longer lives—thanks to medical science. Not every older adult in reset mode is a celebrated path-breaker like Chandy. It could even be the quiet older woman who stays next door, is not creating ripples on social media but is ageing better in her way, through mediums that work best for her.

Ageing Actively

Older is bolder now, and how.

Manjri Varde, sixty-five, is one of them. This Goa-based artist is now an Instagram star with 1,00,000-plus followers and growing. Never hesitant in being herself, Varde sportingly experiments with her daughter-in-law, actor Sameera Reddy, to create content that is not just fun but also turns the age myth on its head. She is the doting grandma one day, the diva with the boots collection on another day and an artist whose creativity is at its peak now, on most days. She doesn't hide her age but it's never a constraining factor in the picture. She's often praised by her followers on Instagram for her friendly and fun relationship with Reddy and her out-of-the box attitude that is ready to pose in a cowboy hat and also play doting grandma. 'As you grow older, it's time for breaking these small false stereotypes we have in our head', Varde tells us, in between stories about driving her daughter-in-law and infant granddaughter to Goa during the pandemic and her wedding-level preparations for making the Gujarati delicacy *undhiyo*. 'It is important to live your life the way you want. I'm sixty-five and for many years I may have done what was expected of me. But in these sixty-five years, I've also learned and gained knowledge and perspective. Now with all of that, if I'm not able to share it, follow it and encourage my entire family, then I'm of no use.'

Ageing is increasingly being seen as a time to redefine oneself. Embracing the advancing years instead of drawing a veil over it seems the new normal—globally. 'The push to embrace ageing as a privilege rather than punishment is starting to feel like a movement,' Carl Honoré writes in *Bolder: How to Age Better and Feel Better About Ageing*.[1] Chronological age is losing its power to define and contain us he says, before sharing examples from New York City to Spain, of older people unafraid to start something new at sixty and beyond. Honoré isn't exaggerating because this is a conversation that's going global. Arnsberg, a city in Germany, even has a Department of Future Aging[2] which looks at creating resources to empower older people to remain active citizens.

We may still be a long way off from creating such next-level systemic resources in India but we are certainly walking there. 'How old would you be if you didn't know how old you are?' says an advertisement by an online shopping aggregator, asking us to #chooseyourage. Old age, at least in the urban Indian environment, is shedding its conventional skin—moving on from the walker to walkathons.

Social change is now reflecting on our screens too. Actor Seema Pahwa recently directed *Ram Prasad Ki Tehrvi*, her first directorial venture at fifty-nine. The movie's elderly protagonist, played by Supriya Pathak, quietly ignores the family arguing about her living arrangements to start a music school in memory of her late husband. Pahwa wrote the movie to reflect the much-needed changes in our mindset around ageing, something that she herself has lived by in her own life by becoming a director in her fifties. 'We need to show more in popular media that there are possibilities to remain independent and productive as you age. It's no coincidence that many films and OTT content are now showing independent older people. It's a reflection of the times we live in.'

The traditional thought that age is time to take a back seat, as the children expect Pahwa's protagonist to do in the movie, is certainly being turned on its head, even if by a minority. People are taking risks, trying out new areas of work and actively pursuing things that will keep their minds buzzing and feet walking as they grow older.

Mirchandani and many others feel this progress is because of several factors. One is the improvement in health parameters due to medical science. The other is the disintegration of society as it was earlier. 'In the joint family there was a clear definition of roles', Mirchandani explains. 'Men went to work and were supposed to retire at a particular age; people had grandchildren around a particular age and women took care of the home. Now we have moved out of the joint family situation, more women are working and roles are no longer strictly defined.' A doting grandmother herself, Mirchandani is there for her close-knit family but maintains her busy work life and social schedule, defining herself by what gives her a sense of purpose.

The Other Side of Ageing

Going by the experiences of Varde and many others, ageing is now being seen as a time to start reliving your life, not just in India but worldwide. Yet, we need to be aware that realities are different for all and many do not view it as a positive life stage.

In March 2020, before the lockdown hit us, we were invited to attend Good Pitch, an initiative by the Indian Documentary Foundation to showcase films addressing social issues and seek support for them. That's where we met Narayan and Irawati Lavate (ninety and eighty-one years, respectively), the first Indian couple to petition the Supreme Court of India for the right to die together with dignity.[3] The Lavates were the protagonists of a documentary being made by film-maker Sumira Roy. As Roy explained the purpose behind her documentary with empathy and optimism for a hopeful future, we saw another very real side to ageing in India. The Lavates petitioned the Supreme Court on their fiftieth anniversary. Roy, who had lost her super active mother recently and was trying to come to terms with it, entered the Lavate's world in their tiny Mumbai chawl, to understand their choice to die.

'They taught me that what matters is how valuable you feel about your place in the world. When I was with them, I felt the silence of loneliness, of isolation, of purposelessness. They are really invisible to the world. And that got me reflecting on how we treat our elders in today's world', Roy said, hoping that her film would be a step towards changing the conversation, and behaviour towards the elderly, and offer pathways for their social re-inclusion.

The Lavates do not have children. They are both largely confined to their small home due to age-related restricted mobility. It may be hard to accept their unusual death wish but not when you understand how lonely and vulnerable life can get for many elders like them. In fact, it stems from life itself—a basic desire to stay independent. The Lavates don't want a future where they are bedridden or unable to manage daily living. They don't want dependence, a worry for many older adults in India. In 2018, when the Lavates petitioned the court, it led to much media debate on the ethical and legal implications of euthanasia. It also showed how diverse ageing itself was. Yes, there were older people around us breaking every ageist stereotype. Yes, active ageing as a concept was certainly a buzzing conversation. But if that was the new truth, so was the reality that for some older people, even death is a better option than being old, ailing and dependant.

Why is that so? Why do we see such disparity?

Consider this. India will have 300 million senior citizens by 2050. Average life expectancy has increased from 56.2 to 70.8 years between 1970–75 and 2013–17.[4] Living longer in a society that is changing rapidly calls for adaptation, something not always easily accessible or possible for many older adults for reasons that range from health, financial, mental and social. It could be one of the reasons the Lavates have chosen the route they did, though it also speaks of their courage in going against the grain. But many older adults are also looking ahead and even embracing the way forward. This book isn't meant to exclude those who aren't redefining age, don't feel the need to adapt or think they've reached the end of a productive life. Its purpose is to look at how we can make the best use of time and resources at our disposal, offer sources of inspiration and bring about empathy when and where required.

Putting Self Ahead

Mohit Nirula, CEO, Columbia Pacific Communities, has observed several older adults and their families as part of his work. He thinks older adults are now putting themselves first. 'People are no longer worrying about leaving large inheritances for their children. The current generation of older adults has become a lot more aspirational than the previous one. People are earning better and, more importantly, they are willing to spend on their lifestyles rather than save.' Nirula thinks that one of the key differences redefining ageing in urban India is not 'the difference in earning but the difference in spending.'

An income increase, together with provident fund, pension and investment measures, has meant better economic solvency for many urban older adults. These self-empowered older adults are clear about their needs and inclined towards fulfilling those.

Madhu Mehra, a Bengaluru-based home entrepreneur, is one of them. Prior to the pandemic, sixty-nine-year-old Mehra travelled regularly with a set of friends in their sixties. Travel helped sustain her after the death of her spouse and continued despite heart and knee surgeries. Mehra isn't alone. In a recent survey by Antara Senior Living, over 65 per cent of seniors chose leisure travel as a 'lifestyle spending preference'.[5] Of course, COVID-19 has thrown a spanner in the works but these figures show the change there is in its willingness to adopt a more active way of life, fuelled by both economics and opportunity.

Mirchandani thinks economic empowerment has made a huge difference. She shares the story of her own parents. 'When they came to India during the Partition from Sindh, they had to start from scratch to rebuild their lives. If you think of Maslow's need hierarchy principle, they were too involved in the lower needs of it (finding food and shelter) to even think of their own fulfilment.' Being economically solvent has changed that for many older adults of Mirchandani's generation, now in their sixties and seventies. 'We're not looking at the basic necessities. We are looking at how we can work to our best potential and self-fulfilment, how we can find out what's good for us and enjoy it; because our stomachs are full and basic needs met.'

Travelling and being part of varied social groups sustained Delhi resident Nirmala Verma after her husband's death. A former economics teacher, Verma travelled both in India and overseas with senior citizens' groups she joined in her middle-class, north Delhi neighbourhood. Becoming a member of senior groups, ladies' clubs, getting involved with activities of the resident welfare association, organizing community activities even through the pandemic has kept Verma busy and mentally alert, the sparkle in her eyes belying her eighty years. When she speaks to us, she highlights that many older adults may just need that little nudge, whether through a peer group or children, to find that self-love and spark of independence that enables them to try new things.

'Joining community groups both mixed age and for elders, opened up my world, increased my social network and gave an all-round development to my personality', she tells us, displaying her latest artwork for us to view. 'I started writing, learnt the harmonium for three years and started trying out creative activities like painting and making videos.' Later in the day, she sends us her vlogs, telling the story of her life, taking a cue from her teenage granddaughter who also makes them. Verma thinks given our longer lifespans, it's essential to focus on keeping one engaged as it helps us deal with the ups and downs that life throws around and keeps us in better health. She also thinks the change in how you react to age and live your older years has gradually come with people of her generation. 'Earlier older people were hesitant to spend on themselves or live their life the way they want. It's changing now all around us, and it is showing in the things we do and explore.'

Older adults like Verma are still following much of the traditional pattern—they saved up to get the kids married;

they babysat grandchildren; many in their sixties and early seventies are even taking care of super senior elderly parents.

The difference now is that they are doing all this and more, but also living life just the way they want, often cheered by their peers.

The Necessities of a New Age

For many older adults, finding that purpose is what keeps ageing and its complexities at bay. What helped Mehra manage loneliness as her husband passed away and her daughters left home, is a knitting venture she started right after retirement. It sustained her emotionally, helped her cope with the loss of her spouse and built intergenerational bonds as she interacted with customers, especially youngsters.

While that purpose came to Mehra through an old hobby, sometimes, it needs to be built in consciously as you grow older.

Dr Tom Verghese is a Melbourne-based author and executive cultural coach of Indian descent who believes in the concept of conscious ageing and actively promotes the idea among older adults globally. 'Conscious ageing is being aware of how I am as a person, going through life and how I'm transitioning through the different stages of life in a positive and active manner', he tells us over a Zoom session from his home in Melbourne, Australia.

How could ideas of conscious ageing help seniors live better and more fulfilling lives as they grow older? Dr Verghese, who has practised it in his own life, says it's being aware of how focusing on aspects of your life like spirituality, physical and emotional health and social connections can help you age better.

Dr Verghese also highlights the importance of having a friendship circle. 'You need friends who are not just of your age group. But ideally, intergenerational friends because they bring different perspectives.' Simply put, conscious ageing is actually enabling people to think they can do something different with their lives as they transition to older age and work towards it.

You may wonder about the importance of a concept like conscious ageing or even wonder why new-age institutes like Modern Elder Academy (in North America and Australia) exist, offering workshops to help people transition to midlife in a positive way. After all, haven't generations of elders around the world and in our own homes lived fulfilling lives without having to read a book on ageing, attend a workshop or even consciously pursue something to make it better?

Perhaps the answer also lies in our fast-transitioning, nuclearized worlds. We may be connected by technology but we are often socially distanced, something your grandfather—who probably lived in a joint family and in a neighbourhood, he had stayed all his life in—may not have experienced. Now, with families spread across the world, and lives often boxed in within apartments, though we are living longer thanks to medical breakthroughs yet are often unconnected from those around us.

Our minds are adapting to a changing world and there are unlimited options around us worth exploring, but we may be held back by generations of conditioning that tells us it's too late to start something new. Our priorities may also have changed, necessitating the need for a conscious transition into elderhood and some of us may need just a bit of handholding to navigate that change.

'What was important for me when I was thirty, may not be important for me when I'm sixty. Position, status and recognition may have been things for me at thirty. Right now, it could be more about how I could be more generous, how I could contribute to the climate change conversation and help make a better world.' Dr Verghese reflects with us.

Akila Krishnakumar would agree. Krishnakumar has been a mentor and guide to us for many years. She is an award-winning former technology industry leader and founding partner of Social Venture Partners, a network of philanthropists. She gave up a corporate top job right at the peak of her career to work with social enterprises, a move that may have been uncharacteristic of her outwardly but deeply fulfilling within. As she tells us about that decision, we realize it is as much carefree thinking as it is a move towards ageing in a conscious way, trying to make the best of the many years ahead of her.

'Work has been my life', says Krishnakumar. 'I couldn't imagine myself sitting at home after retirement. At fifty,

I told myself I have another thirty years of active work in me. If I have to do something with that time, I better get started early.' Krishnakumar was worried that at sixty she may not have enough enthusiasm or energy to start something new. 'I thought if I have to prepare myself for change, I better do it early.' She had reached the top, was long past the financial need to work, had learnt enough on the job and had a great set of experiences to fall back upon. 'Why don't I pluck myself out of the job and do something I really want to do?', she thought. When Krishnakumar quit, the person she surprised most was herself, even if the decision was well-thought-out. 'It took some rashness and that's where the freeing attitude about age comes in', she says.

While Krishnakumar transitioned into a work option she saw herself engaging with purposefully as she grew older in her fifties, senior advocate Shiv Kumar, too, decided to plan a life for himself that went beyond work. Only, in his case, the plan started much earlier.

'I realized very soon that it's pointless being a lawyer, and only a lawyer in your lifetime. We had seen lots of advocates who knew nothing else except law, and therefore found themselves completely at sea when the younger generation began to replace them. And therefore, from the age of twenty-seven, I started developing other habits and hobbies', he tells us. He started working with NGOs which included a helpline for elders that he aided in setting up, pursued theatre alongside and even learned Carnatic music for seven years. 'I cannot sing but can appreciate the music thanks to that', he chuckles. As he grew older, he shifted towards mediation instead of litigation at work as it gave him more satisfaction. Shiv Kumar, who's seventy-three, calls it a very consciously planned growth path. Yes, he does deal with the inconveniences of ageing and loneliness, after the loss of his spouse, still rearing their heads at times. 'That never goes away', he says honestly. But he has tools in his arsenal to enrich the other parts of his life. 'These things—theatre and mediation that I started doing when younger—are holding me in good stead now.'

The Fun and Freedom of Age

Ageing can also often bring with it a certain amount of freedom, a sense of insouciant thinking and the wisdom of being comfortable in your skin. There is something profoundly liberating about ageing, an attitude that is so 'hard-won', says Krishnakumar as she laughs, reminiscing the time when she decided to go grey. 'I just stopped colouring my hair one day. I no longer cared what people thought despite being in a very prominent corporate position at that time. As you grow older, that feeling of being carefree starts to manifest in these little things. You don't feel the necessity to conform. You know you can carry your individuality and you are comfortable with it.'

Mumbai-based costume designer Nyla Masood, sixty-one, has gone grey, too, and like Krishnakumar carries her style with comfort. She often gets mistaken for being much older than her years but faces it with amusement and nonchalance in equal parts. Masood, who turned actor at fifty-eight in director Madhur Bhandarkar's Netflix hit *Liftboy*, sports stylish asymmetric grey hair and rocks the style. She says age has given her a new sense of freedom. 'When I was offered the role in *Liftboy*, I was scared of learning lines but did rehearsals and went ahead.' Now with many films and ads behind her, Masood says being comfortable in her skin helps her get over the nervousness that she still feels initially when offered a role or audition. 'At this stage, I'm not looking for competition or making it big. I'm sure of myself, my self-esteem is at a better level, I know how many challenges I can take and I want to have fun with the roles I get', she says, adding that the grey hair is now part of her look.

Speaking of greys and the carefree freedom age can bring, especially among women, is never more apparent than when you google #ditchthedye.[6] It has become a popular Instagram hashtag with older female influencers celebrating their grey hair and breaking the stereotype that grey equals old. Jin Cruce, who runs the Instagram account @agingwith_style_and_grays, often talks about how difficult transitioning to complete grey hair was. In fact, Cruce says for many women, going grey is part of the pro-ageing movement, which is about embracing and celebrating your age. We would add that it's also about being comfortable in your skin.

Opportunities over Obstacles

Does a carefree mind, conscious planning, self-love and embracing age mean you can avoid worrying about its unavoidable weakening side effects? As the Lavates have shown us, sometimes we may just not be able to. You may have examples in your own circle of someone who is a shadow of their former self at an older age, limited by a weakening body and mind.

Despite advanced medical technology, wearable gadgets and changeable knees, age can still be the biggest debilitating condition of all. It brings with it aches and pains, and as immediate, pressing responsibilities decrease and families become distant and expand, there is a vacuum of connections and sometimes, even a sense of abandonment.

Then there are systemic challenges. The lack of elder-friendly infrastructure is an ongoing concern. Public places like railway stations, bus stands, banks, municipal offices and even religious places are not elder-friendly in India. Crimes against senior citizens, especially in urban India, have been on a steady rise. Reports by the National Crime Records Bureau in 2019 showed that 28,000 seniors above sixty years became victims of crime which also included cases of sexual abuse faced by elderly women. Reports in 2021 show the National Capital Region registering over 900 cases of crime against senior citizens.[7]

Institutionalized support, like in Western countries, is what is missing for elders in India. The social pension system, emergency response, ageing in place (widely used term in ageing policy that defines the ability to live in one's own home and community safely, independently, and comfortably, regardless of age, income or level of ability) and better infrastructure are measures that need to be put in place for a better ecosystem for Indian elders.

As we spoke to older adults in urban spaces across India for this book, we realized that despite the challenges discussed above, we were looking at the 'age of opportunities' enabled by the availability of resources like eldercare organizations working at empowerment and independence, along with dedicated services for elders.

Older adults in India who have access to these resources or the determination to create opportunities for themselves no longer see age as a barrier or view it as a constraint. #AgeNoBar may be an overused social media hashtag, but for many, it truly never comes into the picture.

Sometimes when age is a bar, it can teach us the measures we could take both personally and as a society to make our ageing years better. It means putting systems in place and creating a robust network of support and care which ensure that a lonely older adult can think of an option beyond withdrawing from life and waiting for death.

It is time for us to start looking at age without the lens of an ailment and in a different spirit. Organizations working in the eldercare space are already working towards that—

curating opportunities and resources to ensure ageing can be a positive and healthy life stage with the freedom to explore possibilities.

The conversation has started. Let's keep it going.

2

Keeping Pace: Why Movement Matters with Age

As soon as you feel too old to do a thing, do it.

Margaret Deland, *The Awakening of Helena Richie*

Dr Poonam Bajaj remembers the first time she met Mrs K. She had just started her career as a physical therapist when Mrs K, then seventy-five, told her she would do whatever workout it took, to avoid a knee-replacement surgery. 'It was twenty years ago. When she passed away at the age of ninety-six in 2021, Mrs K was walking and managing movement for daily activities. She never needed that surgery.'

Mrs K did not share her workout on Instagram as an older influencer. She wasn't featured by the media for exercising at eighty. She simply stayed the course. Dr Bajaj, who heads the neurological rehabilitation department in

Mumbai's Sir H. N. Reliance Foundation Hospital, asked Mrs K to use two crutches and walk regularly, apart from doing strengthening exercises. When we speak to her, Dr Bajaj keeps referring to Mrs K as an example, despite having trained senior citizens who have run marathons and had far more fitness 'achievements'. It's because Mrs K's story shows there is no age limit or perfect health condition to start a fitness or movement routine. All you need is the dedication to stick to it. 'Exercise and movement are your biggest anti-ageing elixir', says Dr Bajaj. 'It keeps everything going on, from your heart to skin to your organs. There is no other option to stay active but to incorporate movement in your life, like Mrs K did.'

Are Older Indians on the Move?

Examples of active late-life fitness adapters are all around us these days. Our media has often featured late-life marathoners, sixty-plus mountain climbers, septuagenarian cyclists and octogenarian swimmers. Chandigarh's Tripat Singh, seventy-six, is an Instagram influencer who took up fitness in his sixties to overcome the sorrow of his wife's death.[1] Bylahalli Raghunath Janardan cycles everywhere at eighty-seven, started running after sixty and has completed sixteen full marathons.[2] Supermodel Milind Soman's mother Usha can hold a plank with ease at eighty-one and recently became the oldest Indian to do the Sandakphu trek.[3]

There is a growing interest in starting a fitness routine in many urban elders around us. Mountaineer and former banker Mala Honatti, sixty-seven, organizes trekking expeditions. Most of her clients include older adults, many of them female homemakers who often start working out for the first time only to train for the treks and discover a fitness routine in the process.

It's a great upcoming trend because as we grow older, our physiological functions start ebbing away and movement and exercise become even more important than earlier. Unfortunately, late-life fitness adoptees are a small number, say physical therapists and fitness experts. Usually, the reverse is what happens.

Despite ageing seeing a rewiring in urban India, the common thought is that growing older is a time to rest. Indian homes have help at hand to cook, clean and run errands. This reduces the scope of movement further, especially for older adults. When ailments start appearing, the family's protective instincts kick in—wrapping up the older adult in a cocoon of care and sometimes stopping even the basic activities they are capable of. 'People often forget they can move, or think they are now too old to start', says dance movement psychotherapist Devika Mehta of Synchrony, who has successfully got several older adults to explore movement and enjoy it.

Some years ago, a doctor suggested strengthening exercises and a regular walk to Reshmi's seventy-plus mother. Getting her to do them required the best of her children's convincing powers. 'Why do I need to start exercising at this age?' she countered. This was followed by the surest conversation-ender: 'I cook, I *still* do most of the housework myself. I get enough exercise. Why should I do more?'

Reshmi's mother is active around the house, baking cakes for her grandchildren, gardening and doing much of the daily housekeeping. But experts say a certain amount of exercise or incorporating specific movements in daily activities (discussed later in this chapter) is still required. Of course, it isn't always easy to start something new in your sixties or seventies but it is certainly worth a try.

Human Movement Specialist Badrinath Rao of Bengaluru's Activity Heals explains why. 'As we age, our musculoskeletal strength also takes a beating. This has a significant impact on our daily living activities. When you sit down into a chair or sofa or get up, it is a controlled squat movement; when you climb a slope or stairs, it's a modified lunge. Loss of strength in these areas reduces the amount of power you can generate, making it difficult to do these.'

This reduction in movement could have a domino effect, leading to fear and anxiety about mobility in the mind of the older person, eventual loss of independence and an increase in dependency, impacting overall wellbeing. The solution is simply to move, as much as you are able to, says Rao, who has taught older adults how to manage daily movement and make it fun.

The truth about our ageing bodies may sound like a downward spiral but if you put some work into it, it's actually not. So, if you are wondering if you can get started on a fitness journey despite your senior years, the answer is yes. In fact, it is possible to even run a marathon in Antarctica at sixty-seven if you have the inclination, stamina and training for it. B.R. Hariharan, who is India's second entrant into the prestigious Seven Continents Club (an elite club of runners who have finished marathons in all continents including Antarctica), has done just that. Achievements like his or that of the octogenarian cyclist Janardan are inspirational but these are also the result of determination, the natural wonders of genetics and very hard work. Hariharan worked on strength and cardio training with a group thrice a week. Janardan maintains a strict plant-based diet. So, does this mean you cannot aspire to start a fitness routine or incorporate movement in your life in your sixties if you don't have the same level of stamina or determination? Does it mean doing a brisk walk every day isn't enough? And must movement always mean a fixed set of exercises? As you'll hear from every expert we spoke to, *absolutely not.*

For every senior fitness superstar, there are a growing number of Mrs Ks and neighbourhood park regulars (now probably in a Zoom class) who may not have those uber abs but are diligent with their daily movement routine because they want to keep fit and independent. This chapter will highlight them and how to incorporate fitness and movement into your life to age better.

Persistence Pays and Having a Goal Helps

First, let's meet two movement pathbreakers who chose to pursue fitness in late life systemically. If exercise isn't your best friend yet, their stories can show that even with a health problem and no prior fitness stint, it's possible to get the best out of your body.

Hari Baskaran was an athlete in school, but fitness-related activities decreased as he grew professionally. Baskaran did a reset at sixty. 'I decided to lead an outdoor life and chose cycling as a core fitness activity. I also joined a group of trekkers.' Baskaran pursued his fitness interests even after being diagnosed with myocardial bridge, a congenital heart condition. He adjusted his activities to it, like walking instead of running and cycling on flat surfaces. With gradual cardio training and lung capacity build-up, he has now done high-altitude treks and ultra-marathons, eventually doing a 3,000 km, fifty-eight-day cyclotron from Chennai to Delhi to mark his seventieth birthday. Before the cyclotron, Baskaran's training schedule included a one-and-half-hour cycle ride in the morning and an equivalent time of cardio, strength and flexibility training in the evening. He is an example of using medical guidance and technology to achieve fitness goals, despite a health challenge. 'The best form of training for the heart is to take larger loads gradually. To ensure that I stay within safe limits, I always use a heart-rate monitor when running, cycling or exercising', he says.

P. Geetha, sixty-one, a retired banker from Chennai had not done much beyond regular walks when she went on a beginner's trek to Mizoram and discovered the call of the mountains. She also discovered the need to strengthen her knee. A doctor she met advised popping painkillers until she got that knee replacement surgery. Geetha was appalled. She didn't want surgery and didn't want to keep popping pills either. 'But I knew that I wanted to trek!'

Guided by Badrinath Rao, Geetha, who was fifty-five then, started on a journey of many firsts, pushed by her goal to frequent the mountains. 'I was asked to walk in the swimming pool, and I had never even stepped into one, let alone wear a swimming costume!' Swimming and regular pranayama helped her build lung capacity. Yoga helped with the endurance part. In October 2016, she trekked the Annapurna Circuit, one of the most challenging treks in India. Her story is an incredible one not only because she had never done fitness training before fifty but also because, being an elderly Indian woman who wished to do something offbeat, Geetha faced ageism everywhere—in the gym where the instructors weren't sure if the middle-aged *salwar kameez*-clad lady was serious about strength training and during a trek in Ladakh where the guide wondered if her stamina was up to the 12,000 ft challenge. Each time she handled it with determination and a dose of good humour. 'One of the reasons ageism occurs is because people do not see older people do fitness activities, go on treks, visit the gym or stay active regularly', she told us.

People like Geetha and Baskaran are not outliers. They are simply persistent about achieving their goals. Their achievements speak for themselves and could be a source of inspiration for others to get up and get moving, even with smaller goals.

Sixty-two-year-old Balaka Mitra started yoga for the first time when she was in her mid-fifties. She enjoyed it but the caregiving of super seniors at home and domestic duties meant she couldn't be regular for classes. 'So, I started walking and discovered that I loved it. I had read about the benefits of walking and gradually increased my walking time from fifteen minutes to twenty, then thirty and now I can comfortably walk for forty-five to fifty minutes.' Mitra thinks regular walking has helped her with digestion issues and keeps her mind free of unwanted thoughts. 'I wasn't regular initially as exercise isn't really something my generation was brought up with. I have never seen my mother exercise. But we read a lot about its importance and once I started, I was feeling good and told myself I need to stick to this no matter what.' Now Mitra, who lives in Kolkata, does exactly that. If it rains, she walks in the basement of her building. During the height of the pandemic, when staying indoors was mandatory, she shifted furniture out of the way and walked within her home and then on the building terrace once that opened up. 'I still have enough domestic chores to attend to but it is possible to take out an hour for our health if we are really keen on it.'

Why Should You Get Moving and Start Exercising?

You may not want to climb every mountain like Geetha does or follow a dream of cross-country cycling, but you may wish to keep moving and stay fit, as long as you live.

How would that help you? First of all, it's a preventive practice. Movement reduces muscle loss and functional decline, enabling people to stay active and independent for long.

Sunandha Sampathkumar and Viji Balaji run Growing Young, a preventive healthcare programme for seniors. Before the pandemic and through it, they've run classes (now virtual) for almost ninety older adults with workouts spanning low-impact aerobic exercises to stretching and breathing. The duo face the challenge of convincing older adults to move but the benefits are evident for those who stick to it.

Sampathkumar and Balaji share a common benefit of regular fitness that they've observed from their classes. 'Osteoarthritis is a problem that bothers many Indians. Strengthening exercises from early on helps you stop the conditions from worsening and avoid knee replacement surgery later. With regular exercise and a good diet, you can improve immunity and aim to prevent non-communicable diseases like diabetes, hypertension, and heart disease.'

Exercise also helps your brain create new pathways. You've probably heard the buzz around neuroplasticity, your brain's ability to learn and adapt. Regular physical exercise may help to enhance that and delay the onset of degenerative diseases like Alzheimer's.[4]

It can also help when it comes to falls, the biggest fear for many as they grow older.[5] Did you know that exercising your calf muscles could help you out there? It can facilitate adequate blood circulation to keep your heart healthy, knees stable and improve overall balance, says Dr Bajaj who says moving those muscles are hugely important.

Pro Tip: You can always enrol for balance classes offered by physiotherapists but Human Movement Specialist Badrinath Rao also suggests that elders safely practice the following techniques to get those new neural pathways moving and achieve better balance.

- Standing on one leg (with eyes closed if possible)
- Standing on one leg on a pillow or cushion (only if in a safe zone)
- Standing on one leg while brushing teeth or drinking water (only if in a safe and non-skid surface)

There is a fun side to all this too.

Movement can make you friends. It can also bring a new dimension to your life.

Attending a morning yoga class or walking around the park is also a way to stay socially connected and start the day on a positive note. Post pandemic, some of these activities have moved online but even there, working out with a group is a big motivator.

When Mala Bharath started the dance centre Athmalaya in Chennai and encouraged women who wished to learn dance to join an hour-long weekly training session called Dance Hour, little did she know how popular it would become with many older women.

With their oldest learner in her eighties, Athmalaya's dance programme goes beyond just the traditional routine to enable easier learning. Bharath thinks that learning to dance in the later years has meant enhanced mind-body coordination and more agility for her older learners, many of whom now no longer shy away from showing their skills at family functions.[6] She also thinks memorizing the sequence of steps helps enhance their memory and retention skills, with the camaraderie of group learning adding to it.

Devika Mehta vouches for group work. She has been working with older adults across several health-needs spectrums and has observed its positive effects. 'Increased confidence and communication are what I've seen among people who practice movement regularly. In fact, in a group setting, they start encouraging others who are scared, so that is an added advantage!' Much of Mehta's work has been with people with Parkinson's disease and she has seen numerous instances of positive impact—through group dance therapy. She tells us it has ranged from better expression to improved mobility.

We aren't surprised to hear. Regular exercise can make you happy, even if you start out by thinking of it as a chore. Exercise releases endorphins (the feel-good neurochemicals) and can be a mood lifter for your mind. Studies show that regular exercise increases a brain protein called BDNF that helps nerve fibres grow.[7] Even without the science, the highs of a good workout, whether you sweat it out in a Zumba class or do a good chair-yoga session, are undeniable.

We find that happy factor when we speak to Vijayalakshmi Viswanathan, seventy-four, who went through a lung-related ailment a year ago. Still recovering, she can't stop smiling when she talks about the yoga class she does each week. 'Yoga and pranayam helped improve my lung capacity even after the illness and I can feel the effect all over. I had never thought this would be possible at my age and now I attend the class regularly as much as I can.' Good health can always bring good cheer, and Viswanathan, who wasn't an active exerciser in her younger days and even now only does yoga, is the perfect example of that.

On Your Mark

As every fitness expert exhorts and weightlifting grandpas on Instagram show us, there is no age limit to start an exercise routine. But how much exercise is enough? The World Health Organization recommends 150 minutes of moderate-intensity physical workouts every week for good health benefits. It may seem a lot to someone unused to exercising, but sounds achievable when you break it down: *Do ten minutes of exercise continuously. If you do ten minutes three times a day, that's thirty minutes. Doing that five days a week is 150 minutes.*

Here's what to keep in mind when you start exercising at a later age.

Seek professional guidance and start safe: When taking up a new activity, do it with appropriate monitoring of a qualified physical therapist or fitness trainer. *Always check with your doctor before you start any exercise routine.* Finding the right guide helps, as it did for Geetha. Rao helped build her confidence, never once making her feel that older age and a painful knee meant she couldn't trek.

Start slow: If you have led a sedentary life earlier, then a gradual start is the best way to monitor progress and prevent injuries. Start by walking daily and increase your exercise level steadily.

Pro Tip: Walk for ten minutes at a comfortable pace. Physiotherapists Sampathkumar and Balaji suggest increasing the duration over a few days and finally bringing it to thirty minutes. You can slowly start increasing your speed once you reach that thirty-minute goal.

Know the tools for self-monitoring: How do you know you are doing the right thing? If you do not have any pre-existing health conditions, Dr Bajaj recommends you learn how to self-monitor.

Pro Tip: 'The Borg Rating of Perceived Exertion(RPE)[8] is a simple way of measuring physical activity intensity level and perceived exertion. Ratings between 12 to 14 on the Borg Scale indicate moderate levels of intensity. It is a well-validated and researched scale that corresponds with a safe heart rate region.' If that sounds too complicated, think of it as a simple 'Talk Test', which is holding a short conversation with your walk partner while walking or exercising, without huffing and puffing.

Discover couple goals: There's a reason morning walks are often done in pairs. Find a buddy to share your workout routine with, whether a neighbour or spouse. Encouraging and updating each other on your progress is motivating and keeps you accountable and committed.

Have a goal: Baskaran wanted to do long-distance cycling. Geetha wanted to do tough treks. Mitra wanted to walk for good health and a clear mind. Someone may wish to avoid that knee replacement surgery and keep moving. No goal should be too big or small, experts say. You may not be able to touch your toes in yoga class, but that is no reason to give up. Push your boundaries as much as you can but keep them within the acceptable limits of your body. Having a goal to look forward to makes it easier.

Assistive devices work: The late Mrs K we met in the beginning managed to maintain movement till the end of her life with supervised strengthening exercises and by walking with two crutches.

Very often older adults refrain from using canes or crutches because they don't wish to appear weak. 'The truth is, if the assistive device is keeping you walking, it is in all likelihood keeping you alive and safer from a fall', says Dr Bajaj. 'So don't hesitate to use an assistive device and continue your movement.' Sasanka Chakraborty, seventy-nine, resisted using a walking stick until early 2021 because he didn't want to 'feel old'. Once he started using the stick, he came around despite his reservations— simply because it gave him better balance and confidence. Chakraborty is a regular walker every morning now, his mobility on the rise in the recent months, even if only within his apartment complex in Gurgaon.

Adding Movement to Your Daily Life

If a structured exercise routine is not your thing, there are many ways to consciously incorporate movement in your daily life to stay fit. Some of us often see fitness as something we 'have to do'. The idea is to make it part of our day, with some fun thrown in at times.

Dr Bajaj asks all older adults she works with to stop keeping a bottle of water on their bedside table. 'Keep it in your kitchen or the dining table. Instead of asking someone to do it for you, get up and pour yourself a glass of water at least six times in a day.'

Pro Tip: 'If you are spending your time watching TV and sitting, make sure you do some stretches. If you are sitting on a sofa, kick a ball to the wall back and forth. If you have a grandchild to do it with, it is an additional engagement', says Mehta.

Is housework exercise? Looks like our mothers were right to some extent. If you are largely sedentary at home, start doing manageable housework that is unlikely to cause injury but will get your muscles moving. Pulling out dry clothes (which are lighter) off the clothes rack and folding them is one, as is making your bed every morning or making a cup of tea or mid-morning snack for yourself. These are small habits that go a long way to keep you moving and get you out of a sedentary zone. You could even take inspiration from Idea Cellular's popular ad campaign 'Walk n Talk', of 2009, where you could walk while talking on your phone, adding up to your step count for the day.

Pro Tip: Rao shares fun routines most older adults could get going to add more movement to their life.

- Roll in the bed from one side to another but keep your stomach and buttocks tight. It improves core and spine strength.
- Walk in the pool if you have access to one and can do this safely. It's a great activity to improve cardiovascular health.
- Learn to crawl like a baby on all fours on the floor or on the bed—it teaches you spinal balance and improves strength in the upper body.
- Stand up against the wall with heel, buttocks, shoulder blades and back of your head touching the wall for one minute every hour. It improves your awareness of correct posture and prevents the strain on your spine.

What to Pick When You Are Exercising

If you are all set to get fit, the choices available are plenty. Yoga, tai chi, qigong, low-impact aerobic exercises, swimming, aqua aerobics, walking, interval jogging (walking and jogging alternated), dancing, cycling are all various forms of exercises older adults can take up, based on interest, availability and convenience.

Pro Tip: If you wish to pursue specific high-activity goals, Dr Bajaj suggests a biomechanical evaluation—a critical analysis of your body and its moving parts.

Walking: The easiest and most achievable exercise for older adults is walking. The best way to get cardiovascular health benefit is sixty minutes of walking at a sustained pace (The Talk Test applies here too). You can break it down to thirty minutes each in the morning and evening.

Here's a fun tip to add more to that regular walk: Start by keeping ten numbered stones in your hand. Every few minutes, place a stone by the footpath or in a bush and continue walking until you have kept the tenth one. On your way back, trace your steps and pick up your numbered stones. This exercise helps with memory and spatial awareness.

Dance Movement Therapy: This form of psychotherapy uses movement to process emotional and behavioural health. Movement psychotherapist Devika Mehta says the biggest benefits include an exponentially increased confidence, letting go of inhibitions, better communication and the scope for expression, even if it may take some convincing for older adults to do some footwork. 'With dance, they're able to tell you what they are feeling or experiencing. And that ability to express is very rarely provided within the scope of elderly space.'

Yoga: The best thing about yoga is that 'it meets you where you are at', says yoga practitioner and trainer Sujata Cowlagi. If you're starting out in your fifties or sixties, then it's advisable to start with a practice that is not too laborious or difficult and gradually step up. 'Joint-loosening practices done with elders may appear very simple, like making rotations with your wrists. But these are useful because they remove the rigidity in specific joint areas. And that provides you the springboard to go towards more intricate practices.' If done right, yoga—a holistic and sustainable practice—can be done lifelong at a pace that works for the elder, says Cowlagi, based on the concept of *yatha shakti* or individual capacity. Chair yoga, an accessible form of practice, is very beneficial, the biggest benefit being the accessibility and inclusivity it offers to older adults who may find it difficult to sit on the floor and hence avoid practice.

Zumba Gold: Into more energetic activities? If you like dance, and movement isn't an issue, then new-age workouts like Zumba Gold feature the Latin American-inspired styles of regular Zumba in this low-impact version. Benefits include a happy mood with all that dopamine and serotonin secretion, weight management and better cognitive function, given the hand-eye coordination required in Zumba moves. *Remember that you need to practice this only after checking with your doctor and always under the guidance of a licensed Zumba Gold instructor.*

Qigong: Qigong, an ancient Chinese healing modality and meditative practice, can be ideal for elders with its gentle, meditative moves. It can help improve balance, eyesight, coordination and flexibility, says Malini Mundle, sixty-eight, who has been practising it for thirteen years. Mundle says it has also helped improve her breathing and focus. Qigong uses slow graceful movements and controlled breathing techniques to promote the balance of yin and yang by coordinating the mind, body, breath and chi or energy to enhance overall health. 'The purpose of the postures and movements of qigong is to regain the balance between body, mind and spirit and achieve harmony and balance physically, mentally and emotionally', Mundle adds.

How do we find the right classes and instructors, virtual or otherwise? Connect with senior citizen groups and clubs in your city who may be running fitness classes for older adults or lead you to dedicated movement experts. (Check for the resource guide at the end of the book.)

Starting to work out helped Geetha not just get closer to the mountains she loved so much but also deal with loneliness. She now trains for three hours each day, does yoga, apart from walking regularly, and strongly advocates late-life fitness, even if done at a moderate level for the invaluable mind-body wellness it brings.

'I live alone but don't feel depressed. I can always go for a walk to change my mood. Fitness has had a huge positive impact on me mentally. It has given me something to look forward to.'

What she says is a throwback to the senior dancers at Athmalaya who now practise dance daily and have been able to incorporate a joyful movement regularly in their lives. It has created a 'me-time' routine for many of them, given them a conversation starter and made them feel capable and energized, besides getting them started on a movement practice. It's an assertion of the fact that fitness need not be limited to big medal-hauling achievements or a particular form of exercise. Most importantly, getting fit can begin at any age and is not a single-sized fit.

It's a reminder to get up, get moving and engage our bodies. The mind shall follow.

3

The Mind Map: Learn to Be Kind to Your Mind

To keep the heart unwrinkled, to be hopeful, kindly, cheerful,
reverent—that is to triumph over old age.

Thomas Bailey Aldrich

Daddy had always been Sangeeta John's world. John, a Mumbai-based former journalist, lost her mother at an early age. Her father was a single parent and a mining engineer who raised her with love and affection and retained his sharp and analytical mind well into post-retirement. When he repeatedly started to complain about physical ailments that seemed to have no solution despite umpteen doctor visits and distancing himself from her, John sought out psychological help. Eventually, her father was diagnosed with anxiety.

John has always been an aware daughter, clued to her father's health needs. Yet it took her time to get the right diagnosis for her father, because everyone—including her—focused on his physical health first.

John isn't alone. Our friend Shoma realized she had to pay as much attention to her father's mental well-being as she did to his hypertension and vision problem when he was hospitalized for delirium some years ago. Her father had an eye operation and once back home showed increasing signs of paranoid behaviour. He was seventy-six, not always the best of patients and Shoma thought it was the quirks of age and illness-related discomfort. The fact that it could have a mental-health connection was far from her mind.

Geriatric psychiatrist Dr Santosh Bangar isn't surprised when we shared this with him. As one of the few trained liaison psychiatrists[1] for older adults in India, Mumbai-based Dr Bangar works closely with general physicians in hospitals and often comes across older adults who have auditory and visual hallucinations, like Shoma's father. He says we seldom realize that imbalanced physiological parameters can also manifest as mental-health issues and vice versa. 'ICU psychosis or delirium is a state of acute confusion, where older adults can become aggressive, agitated, paranoid and hallucinate because of physical imbalances. It is extremely common.'

In our classic focus on physical health, more so for older adults, we often forget that the mind needs as much care and attention as does the body. With older people, problems can run the risk of being brushed away under the carpet of 'old-age issues' even by the most empathetic families.

We couldn't be more wrong.

Geriatric psychiatrists say the most common mental-health issues they come across in older adults are depression, delirium, anxiety-related issues and disorders related to substance abuse and addiction, lack of sleep and chronic pain. In fact, 30 per cent of the 103 million people above sixty in India have symptoms of depression, says the 2021 Longitudinal Ageing Study (LASI).[2]

Neurodegenerative conditions like dementia, epilepsy and Parkinson's disease may manifest as mental-health issues for years, say experts. 'Sometimes people may come with anxiety, sleep problems, constipation, loss of sense of smell or nightmares, before being diagnosed with a neurological condition,' Dr Bangar adds.

What is a good state of mental health? Mental-health experts we spoke to for this book, describe it not just as the absence of a disorder but a state of emotional well-being where you are able to cope with challenges that life may throw your way. And while everyone experiences some form of stress, it is an individual's response to it that determines the extent and need for counselling and intervention. If you are a caregiver to an older loved one, what you need to remember is that the signs of deterioration in functioning are often more apparent to others than the individual himself. As experts point out, a compassionate approach is the key to helping them make meaning of this experience.

Ageing isn't an easy process in a world where the pandemic has turned long-held social norms and ways of living upside down. Devoid of their usual routine and a looming sense of an uncertain future, many older adults are trying hard to adapt to the 'new normal'.

'I couldn't believe how much my mum had aged in the last one year when we met after thirteen months!' a friend shared, concerned that her once-outgoing parent who went to the gym and bank like clockwork and met friends regularly before the pandemic, put a stop to it, and did not have much to look forward to. 'I can see a disinterest and lack of positivity and that's worrying.'

More than ever, it is time to pay attention to the mind as much as we do to the body, as it ages. Even the data says so. The National Mental Health Survey conducted by NIMHANS in 2015–16,[3] showed that 10.9 per cent elderly were in need of mental health care. Worryingly, the treatment gap[4] was 85 per cent, showing the apathy towards mental-health treatment in India.

The Pandemic Change

All the above data is hard-hitting but doesn't always translate into action in terms of seeking help. But in an unexpected way, the pandemic has helped the cause of mental healthcare in India where data and studies haven't. COVID-19 made social isolation and loneliness huge challenges for older adults. It was a big blow for many who had enjoyed their daily morning walks, trips to the vegetable vendor, visits to family or evening chats with friends in the neighbourhood park, to stay isolated at home with no community interaction for over a year and more. It did not just impact their emotional stability and routine—the constant talk about older people being the most vulnerable to the virus only added to their distress.

The downsides were obvious but the unprecedented situation also led to many older adults and their families opening up to counselling.

In 2020, a mental-health helpline for senior citizens run by Agewell Foundation, an elder empowerment non-profit, started getting eighty to 100 calls daily compared to the ten it received earlier. It was a significant rise, according to Himanshu Rath, the founder of Agewell, given the backstory of mental-health taboo and unawareness. The high level of reaching out to the helpline showed a growing cognition towards seeking support, not just from older adults but also their families. Rath told us that several calls came from worried children.

Sandhya Rajayer calls it a welcome change. The Bengaluru-based mental-health therapist has counselled many older adults through the pandemic and says children, many of whom would have observed their parents closely when sharing the same space for months, are encouraging them to reach out. 'The pandemic has made even the older generation open to the possibility of seeking support. Older people are taking help from professional therapists, encouraged and, in some instances, financially supported by their adult children.'

Why Opening Up Helps

Very often older adults look at emotional distress as a sign of weakness or wonder how it could happen to them.

'I've handled so much in life, I don't need a doctor to feel better!' A caregiver has often heard this from his disbelieving parent, who has clinical depression and wonders why this has happened to him. Many older adults tell their doctor they don't have a history of psychological illness in the family and hence don't think 'it can happen to them'.

The opposite is often true. Mental-health experts say that often behavioural and psychological disorders could be triggered by traumatic life events like loss and other grief, genetic predisposition, loneliness, loss of purpose during a life transition like retirement, and physical imbalances, among other reasons.

But recognizing and accepting support can lead to timely diagnosis of problems and a better quality of life. Manjima Moitra, sixty-seven, is trying to do just that. Moitra spent the first half of 2020's lockdown cooking, reading, calling up old friends and trying to stay as active as she could. Then the worrying started, a constant feeling from morning to night, gnawing away at her. Gradually it started clouding everything, especially when Moitra started having intense digestive health issues. 'I didn't want to talk to people or do too many things which was surprising for an extrovert like me,' she tells us. Eventually, Moitra was diagnosed with Generalized Anxiety Disorder (GAD), also the cause behind her digestion troubles. What makes her different is the openness she showed towards working on her mental health even if the diagnosis came as a surprise. 'I consider myself fairly well-informed but didn't know that anxiety could be at the root of my physical problems. But now that it is diagnosed, I am actually relieved and working towards better health.'

What stops many from being open like Moitra is the quiet demon of stigma that needs to be tackled head-on.

Stigma is the reason why the silver-haired Kalpana Rao, fifty-eight, opens up about her life on Instagram and Clubhouse. It's hard to believe that this cheerful actor contemplated taking her life during a dark phase of depression not too many years ago. Recognizing that she needed to seek mental-health support, talking openly about it with her husband and working on her fitness helped Rao, who doesn't shy away from speaking about her struggle. She thinks following a hobby or passion always helps and consciously spreads that message, especially among elders. 'I try to encourage a lot of older people to work on something that they are passionate about. For some, it could be yoga, for some painting, for some gardening or knitting.' Rao also credits her fitness routine with helping bring back her emotional balance and self-love.

When to Seek Help: Identify the Red Flags

Most of us are aware of dementia and Alzheimer's disease, a neurodegenerative condition that affects an estimated 3.7 million Indians over sixty. But despite media talk and presumed awareness around it, dementia is still mired in misinformation and stigma, like most mental-health issues are. The biggest problem in seeking help, says neuropsychologist Tanvi Mallya remains early detection. Mallya runs a mental-health service for older adults, specializing in neurodegeneration, in Mumbai. She says one of the major checkpoints in the detection of all mental-health issues remain elders themselves. They may not report an ongoing condition to their family or physician due to embarrassment or lack of awareness, attributing it to normal ageing instead. However, there seems to be a slight shift in this trend, given the fallout from the pandemic and the lockdowns and the heightened awareness and focus on mental health in general.

In the case of dementia, often families only approach doctors after something goes wrong, such as an older adult wandering off and forgetting the way back home or getting agitated at frequent intervals, a behaviour change that continues over a period of time. 'Families remain unaware of warning signs because of our focus on physical problems,' says Mallya. 'Be observant. For example, you may notice an elder cutting out activities that involve walking around and these may all be signs of a loss of spatial reasoning, which often shows up a lot before the short-term memory loss in dementia.'

Experts say that a good point of initial referral could be a general practitioner who may then direct you to a neurologist, psychologist, psychiatrist or social worker for clearer answers.

How do you know if a parent's persistent sadness or decreased interaction is a sign of neurological degeneration or deeper emotional distress? How do you know when to seek help for mental health? Act on your instinct and seek medical help if you feel something is off, says John, who has followed that through her caregiving journey.

John has been a caregiver for almost ten years now, and if like her, you have been a caregiver too, you'll probably recognize many of the hurdles she talks about—lack of early diagnosis, managing a senior citizen's physical and emotional setbacks, explaining decisions to often contrary family members and trying hard to create a conducive environment for the elder. Caregivers like her believe we need to be alert towards all possible warning signs so that care needs are detected early.

Here's a checklist of mental-health red flags we collated after speaking to caregivers and experts. Remember that the signs may not follow the same pattern for all but if some of these happen consistently, a doctor visit could be due.

- Changed sleeping pattern—either too less or too much
- Unexplained loss of weight or weight gain
- Lack of appetite or disinterest in eating
- Choosing to become socially isolated; avoiding usual activities like a club meeting; Disinterest, apathy or withdrawal from people at home or social network.

- Lack of interest or unwillingness to do activities the older adult regularly did and enjoyed.
- Self-neglect in terms of grooming, avoiding medication or check-ups consistently
- Indulging in uncharacteristic intoxication or substance abuse
- Instances of short-term memory loss like forgetting where things are kept or asking for food even after eating; being repetitive about incidents.
- Hypochondria or constant worry about ailments
- Inability or disinterest in learning new things
- Frequent and unexplained mood swings

Where to Go When There's a Problem

Baroda-based Shyamli Pathak's father Amit, sixty-seven, has vascular dementia, brought on by a massive stroke three years ago. When she and her mother realized his memory-related problems, they were initially clueless about the next step. It's a common dilemma for many. You know where to go if Dad gets high blood pressure but where do you take him when it could be connected to the mind?

A specialized practitioner like a neurologist or psychiatrist would be a good starting point.

You could also approach services like Mallya's that guide the family on care systems to be put in place to help older loved ones age better. She recommends regular health screenings, including brain scans, even if done every alternate year, given the high level of expense. She also agrees that finding the right treatment could take time. 'There is a lot of ageism that also interferes with diagnosis, both in families and medically. Sometimes even a physician may put down certain conditions to old age. Assessments like a brain scan give us a more tangible picture of what's really at play and if there's something, the steps to manage it.'

Mallya says, culturally, most Indians resist spending on any service that does not fit their predetermined view of essential medical help or quick relief. 'Mental health is not seen as that kind of need.'

But more than in the medical environment, ageism routinely occurs within families the most. As John talks about her experience, she urges us to write this: 'If you have a senior at home who doesn't seem to be well for some time, don't give up easily on them and dismiss things by saying it's nothing but age-related.'

The need to create awareness about mental-health treatment has seen a lot of recent media attention, including using the right terminology.

The Centre for Brain Research at The Indian Institute of Science in Bengaluru has a long-running study on Alzheimer's that aims to map the rate of decline of cognition in people above forty-five.[5] The study already has 450 volunteers across the city. The institute recently launched a mobile unit to go across the city for testing purposes.

Celebrities like Deepika Padukone have openly spoken about their mental-health issues. Mediaperson

Faye D'Souza often speaks about the need for self-care breaks. However, it is still rare to find older adults who are vocal and affirmative about the need to take care of your mind. Even if you come across some who do, finding the right resources and creating an impact with that awareness remains a challenge. If we are open to it, there's help at hand. Five out of every 100 elderly in India have dementia and many more are at high risk of developing this condition, says the Alzheimer's & Related Disorders Society of India (ARDSI), which works towards providing medical and caregiving support for dementia. There are now several dementia support groups across India that you could seek help from, even online. Many practitioners regularly guide elders and families towards resources that can help them keep their minds functioning sharp and active—whether it is a senior citizens' club offering enrichment activities or a support group for people with Alzheimer's and dementia.

Wondering how to find these resources? Ask your doctor. Approach organizations like ours that work with senior citizens. They usually have a handy list of support services and could help you find one in your city. Some organizations, including ours, offer phone-buddy support, where a volunteer regularly connects to enquire after an elder's emotional well-being.

You can dial 14567—a toll free number called Elder Line, which is a National Helpline for Senior Citizens that works through the week to provide information on medical services, legal aid, intervention and emotional support, among others.

Contacting healthcare non-profits is another way to find out resources like dementia day-care centres, community centres for active ageing and support groups. A Google search or looking up specific groups on Facebook can also be helpful. The resource guide for this chapter (at the end of the book) has information on the same.

The Mind Blockers: Mental-Health Roadblocks

In Shoojit Sircar's *Piku*, Amitabh Bachchan's character displays death- and health-related anxiety, sensitively reflective of what many older people and their caregivers experience. The mental health of older adults has recently found empathetic, inclusive voices in India's popular culture, a welcome change that hopefully is coming to represent a slow normalization. Dementia and Alzheimer's disease have been sensitively portrayed in some Hindi and regional-language cinema,[6] like *Maine Gandhi Ko Nahi Mara*, *Astu* and *Mayurakshi*.

But the stigma remains, especially among older adults, conscious or unconscious. Pathak's mother hasn't revealed her father's dementia diagnosis to most of their relatives. She fears it will hamper her daughter from getting marriage proposals. 'There is still a huge stigma around it, especially in smaller towns,' says Pathak, who finds it hard to convince her mother.

Few days after we speak to Pathak, we meet Wendy Mitchell from UK on a Zoom webinar. Diagnosed with Early-Onset Alzheimer's at fifty-eight, Mitchell—now sixty-five—can be called an awareness ambassador for dementia. When she realized the lack of awareness around dementia globally, Mitchell started writing a blog and giving awareness talks of how she tries to outmanoeuvre the disease daily.[7] Sadly, it's hard to find an Indian Wendy Mitchell. Persons with dementia are rarely open about it, and there is no incorporation of their voices in any advocacy or awareness issues, says Swapna Kishore, a former caregiver who is a key dementia resource person in India and runs one of the best Indian resource websites for it—dementiacarenotes.in.[8] Kishore thinks the main reason, apart from stigma, is the late detection of cases, by when the person is likely to be in mid-stage dementia, with associated problems.

Financial challenge is the other dampener to mental-health support in India. Therapy sessions cost anywhere between Rs 1000 to 2000 and above, an amount very few older adults can afford on a regular basis.

The lack of insurance coverage is a hindrance too. After the passing of the Mental Healthcare Act 2017, the Insurance Regulatory and Development Authority of India (IRDAI) mandated insurance coverage for mental-health conditions in the same way as physical health.[9] Though some insurers offer products customized to this guideline now, most of the cover is only for hospitalization, which is rare. The lack of financial cover can have a negative impact, say families and mental health experts, especially in long-term conditions where an older adult may need a respite care facility. Nidhi faced this challenge when her mother gave up on counselling after three sessions after finding out what the cost for each session was. Nidhi saw it as an emotional well-being necessity but her mother, like many elders in India, felt it was an expense that wasn't required. 'What the counsellor is suggesting I am aware of it already. She cannot solve my personal issues', she reasoned.

One route many psychiatrists take to work around this challenge is to connect the symptoms to physiology and make the treatment more acceptable to an older adult using the medical model.

Dr Soumya Hegde, a geriatric psychiatrist from Bengaluru who has worked across eldercare centres and dementia care groups, suggests a gentle way of explaining to older adults that they may need therapy for emotional wellbeing. 'As human beings, we all have a tendency to be affected. We try to surround ourselves with positive thoughts and positive people but when we find ourselves overwhelmed by our own emotions, that is the time to seek help.' It is perhaps a good way to guide an older adult who may see psychological support as a sign of weakness.

The most common question Dr Hegde is asked by her patients is if their problem can be treated without medication and if medication is addictive. She explains why it may be needed. 'The level of disability one experiences as a result of psychiatric illnesses like anxiety or depression varies from person to person. To be able to engage in counselling, or therapy and be motivated to work on the suggested strategies is not always possible when one is ill. These medicines undergo rigorous clinical trials. They are not experimental drugs. They treat the illness and enable people to live a better quality of life.' Increasing awareness about these aspects also helps to go around the resistance in elders' minds that mental-health issues are real. Though the fact that these are not measurable in the conventional ways makes the fight a little harder.

How to Be Kind to Your Mind

One of the kindest acts you can do for your mind is to find a sense of purpose. In the global bestseller *Ikigai: The Japanese Secret to a Long and Happy Life,*[10] the authors share examples of this across Japan, especially in Okinawa, the village with the highest number of centenarians, showing how finding your *ikigai* or a sense of purpose can keep you focused and enhance emotional well-being. Your sense of purpose could be a hobby, activities you do around the house, a vocation or a cause. It could be using your skills to teach underprivileged children like Charles Narayanan, a retired radiation physicist in Bengaluru, does.[11] Lovingly called Tuition Uncle, Narayanan says teaching helps him keep his mind sharp, utilize his skills and gives him something purposeful to wake up for, every morning. His first student, Pooja, who barely knew English, Math or Science when she started, finished a Bachelors in Computer Application degree in 2021 and secured a job in a reputed IT firm. Narayanan says such success stories keep him motivated to do more and his mind functioning actively.

Exercising the brain helps too. We have all read about the cognition-sharpening powers of Sudoku. Cognitive activities like solving a puzzle, doing a word game, crafting or learning something new keep the brain working. Chennai's Suguna Rangaswami, eighty-two, attributes much of her mental agility to her love for crafting (she makes soft toys and puppets), Scrabble and other word games that she has played over the years. If games like Scrabble improve brain plasticity, experts also suggest learning a new language or instrument or trying something new such as gratitude journaling. Brain gym exercises can also help the brain develop new connections.

Sleep, as neuropsychologist and sleep scientist Matt Walker puts it, is your life-support system. A study conducted by Walker showed that older people above sixty had almost 70 per cent loss of deep sleep compared to people less than twenty-five. As Walker says in his now-famous TED talk, disruption of deep sleep may contribute to cognitive decline and Alzheimer's disease as well.[12] So, sleep as well as you can. Your brain will thank you for it.

For some, it's spirituality that helps achieve emotional stability, especially in a world battered by negative news and grim happenings. Meditation, chanting, devotional music, becoming part of a spiritual study group or motivational texts may help find a space of calm and healing. Our next chapter on spirituality explores this further.

One day, Moitra calls to tell us about trying out meditation apps like Calm and Insight Timer. These apps offer short guided meditations and music that is aimed at helping people unwind, relax and help first-timers navigate ways to meditate. It's not something she has done earlier. She would have watched the news or been on social media instead, something she now avoids. 'I still don't find meditation very easy but I'm trying my best. I'm gradually learning how to feel better', she says, her quest for a better quality of life shining through.

It reminds us that our emotional imperfections and struggles could be like the Japanese art of Kintsugi—where precious metals like gold are used to give broken ceramics a beautiful new look. We don't need to hide the broken parts within us—instead, we can be aware of their fragility, learn to work with them and emerge stronger. It's a long road ahead in the journey of opening up to mental health in India, but as older adults like Moitra and caregivers like John show us, acceptance among the elderly has gradually begun.

4

The Spirit Within: How Spirituality Can Help

Wisdom comes with winters.

Oscar Wilde

'It was the tenth day in captivity since my husband and I had been abducted by militants as a bargaining chip for the release of twelve terrorists. I had been crying all night and couldn't sleep. At the sound of the morning azan of the first namaz of the day, I found myself in an angry dialogue with God for having subjected us to this ordeal and questioning His very existence. I was crying copiously and feeling all the venom that had accumulated in my system over the last few days. I felt like a hand grenade that could blow up the group if I could just lay my hands on a weapon! I wanted to kill them all! As I continued this bitter exchange, slowly and subtly a change started to come over me. The lump in my throat that had felt like a solid block of ice started melting', shares Khem Lata Wakhlu about an experience in 1991, at the peak of militancy in Kashmir. 'At the crack of dawn as light started streaming into the room, for the first time, I looked at the faces of the militants sleeping around us, one by one. At that moment a shift happened and I saw them as helpless fellow human beings. I experienced forgiveness and letting go.'

Wakhlu is an author and a political and social activist from Srinagar, Kashmir.

The transformational experience that night shifted her outlook, making her bolder around the militants, sometimes donning the role of a teacher, scolding them for their wayward ways and even finding the courage to slap one of them. 'I always believed that both of us would return home unscathed, which we did after spending forty-five days in captivity, moving across seventy hideouts until we were rescued by the Indian Army. My meditation practice and positive belief helped us see it through.'

Wakhlu and her husband convinced the militants to surrender their arms when they were surrounded by the army personnel on the forty-fifth day. The militants returned to the village and mingled with the crowd avoiding any bloodshed, saving the lives of the villagers who had given them shelter.

What was that transformation that came over Wakhlu? What she experienced can only be described as a shift in her inner spirit or soul. The mind, body and soul are like the trinity of our lives. In the previous chapters we spoke about taking care of our body and mind, but what about our soul? In this chapter, we talk about this final piece of the jigsaw puzzle called healthy and active life.

What is a soul? The way we interpret it, it's the deep connection between the mind and the body—like the energy that courses through an electrical circuit and lights up a bulb. To activate that energy, you need to connect or plug in to the source of electricity. Spirituality is that nourishing source for our soul.

Many understand spirituality as the connection with the divine, God or a higher power. But through our conversations, we found that even an atheist can be spiritual, for spirituality transcends religion.

Maitreyi Dadashreeji, the spiritual guide of MaitriBodh Parivaar[1] explains, 'In life, religion conveys the message of truth, teaching us how to practically apply spirituality. However, with time, it has become lifeless and mechanical. Socially and politically influential people altered religious essence and ways to suit their agenda and position in society. As a result, we ended up with conflicts between the spiritual path and religious teachings. Simply put, being religious is about a priest's relation with the deity's statue, whereas being spiritual is about the connection between a devotee and their beloved Lord. Spirituality connects you with the divine, and religion creates society to follow a spiritual path. Religion may bind you, if misunderstood. Spirituality sets you free.'

'If we were to think of religion as a cluster of thoughts, beliefs, rituals, patterns and world views that ostensibly takes a person to a god, wholeness and joy, then we can think of religions as different windows, each having its own colours and structures. But spirituality is that sky to which all these windows open. Spirituality is the sky of wholeness, peace, oneness, deep joy and freedom'. says Arun Wakhlu, the Founder Director of Pragati Leadership and an author, coach and master facilitator in the area of Wholesome Leadership TM.[2]

Nithya Shanti,[3] a spiritual teacher and guide who led a monastic life for six years, says we are all spiritual. 'Spirituality is religion minus fear. Religion is more the outer crust, the exoteric and the spirituality is esoteric, the inner essence. We typically have to start with the outer end, start with beliefs and dogmas, question them little by little, and finally, we come to the essence of it. At the outer level, religions look so different—how a pineapple cake looks different from a chocolate cake and a strawberry cake. However, the spongy material inside is the same for all cakes. Similarly, religions look different on the outside, but their inner essence is actually the same. Religion is the mind, spirituality is the heart, and we are making this journey. The pilgrimage from the head to the heart is the longest journey in the world.'

Spirituality is very personal and can manifest in different forms, and there is no wrong way to do this. For some, it may be their sense of purpose, while for others it may be just daily practices that keep them grounded and in touch with themselves. For Nidhi's mother, it is about her connection with the divine. Her daily practice of meditation, puja, listening to bhajans and discourses and most importantly, her faith in the higher power, keeps her connected with herself and shielded from the negative stimulus that may come from her external environment sometimes. For Arun Wakhlu, his spiritual practice includes taking short pauses through the day and focusing on his breath, becoming mindfully aware of the present. Between the two of us, Nidhi prefers meditation, attending spiritual workshops and listening to her spiritual teacher, while for Reshmi it's her chanting practice at the end of the day that brings her peace and balance.

Spirituality is within us and Wakhlu suggests an easy way to access it. 'We have been granted a beautiful emotional guidance system that allows us to navigate our life by the way we feel. When figuring out what to do next or your purpose of life or when stranded or confused, apply the JEEP test where J = Joy, E = Energy, E = Enthusiasm and P = Peace. If your action is going to bring you all of this, you are on the right path.' His spiritual sadhana includes engaging in activities that pass the JEEP test. He loves going trekking, engaging with family and friends and conducting his wholesome workshops. For Heera Rupani, her sense of service passes the JEEP test. She nourishes her soul by serving others and this is her daily practice. 'I make sure I feed the needy the same food that I would feed my family. There is no difference. If I would eat a Rs 20 samosa I would feed the same samosa to others. I would not fulfil my mission of being of service by feeding them a lower quality samosa,' says Rupani. Her service goals are accompanied by her daily rituals of lighting the lamp, reading scriptures, chanting and meditation. 'I do these practices not out of binding to my religion or any fear or superstition. I do them because they give me joy and peace,' adds Rupani. Shiv Kumar, a senior advocate in Karnataka High Court, also finds his deepest spiritual practice in doing pro-bono work, offering mediation services to help people resolve issues without having to go to court. 'The question that I ask myself is "how can I help" and not "do I want to help",' says Kumar.

What Is the Role of Spirituality in Our Life?

Spirituality primarily provides two things—being present in the moment and letting go of the past! When the past doesn't haunt you, you instantly attract joy. Positivity, acceptance and a happy mind become a significant part of your life. Simply enjoy life! Spirituality helps you accept the situation as it is. No matter how bad or good it is! You are fully present in that moment with no complaints.

—Maitreyi Dadashreeji

Famous Bollywood actor Suresh Oberoi had an illustrious acting career and led a life of name, fame and showbiz until a tragedy changed the course of his life. Oberoi lost his brother in a car accident while travelling from Hyderabad to Mumbai. He blamed himself for the loss as it was upon his insistence that his brother had accompanied him on that fateful day. His world was broken and he turned towards spirituality to seek answers to questions that the impermanence of life had triggered in him. He found refuge and solace with his first spiritual Guru Dada Lakshmi. Then his introduction to Brahma Kumaris and Sister Shivani[4] during the TV show 'Happiness Unlimited' that he hosted, cemented his spiritual path. 'Spirituality transformed me forever. I lost my anger. From being madly angry I turned to being hardly angry. I gave up my vices, turned vegetarian. My heart health improved. I even lost my glasses. I was a changed man.' Such was the transformation that a few years ago when a family member insulted him at a party, Oberoi reacted with no reaction at all and even gifted the person with a present as he found himself forgiving and distant from the situation.

Jaishree Kannan grew up in her maternal grandparents' home after her mother moved back with her parents when Kannan was a little girl. Kannan knew nothing about what had happened with her father and why they were living with her grandparents. She grew up listening to Vedanta from her grandfather and had a fairly comfortable life. Well-educated, she found a good job and married into a wonderful family. Everything was comfortable till she discovered she had cancer. It hit her badly. She started losing all interest in life. She became depressed and started pulling back from family and friends. One day a friend brought her a book *You Can Heal Your Life* by Louise Hay,[5] insisting that Kannan should read it. Kannan kept resisting reading the book until one fine day she felt the urge to try it out. 'I sat with the book for hours and finished reading it at a stretch. That book shifted something in me and made me realize I had always been unhappy. I had been festering anger towards my father for deserting us and that I had to heal myself by forgiving him and myself.' This cleared up Kannan's inner environment making her more receptive to her treatment, fast-tracking her to becoming cancer-free.

Rupani grew up in a family that believed in doing service unto others. She had been in the practice of engaging in activities for the benefit of others since a young age. She is also a devotee of Dadaji of Sadhu Vaswani mission. Four years ago, she had a major setback when she lost her husband out of the blue on his birthday. 'We had a small family gathering at our Hyderabad home and had just finished dinner. Suddenly I heard my husband coughing incessantly in his room. We rushed him to the hospital but lost him on the way. In that moment of tragedy, I found myself in full control of the situation. I along with my children informed friends and family and I personally made arrangements to do his last rites at Dadaji's ashram in Pune. I found strength in my spiritual practices and my faith, and it helped me accept the loss and cope better.'

Kumar has a similar story to share. 'When I lost my wife, I kept asking why did it happen to me, for a while, until a friend asked me one day, why not you? This question snapped me out of my misery and helped me accept the reality of things beyond my control. Memories still come up and I just let them run their course. I find solace in my practices and my work.'

All the above examples tell us that spirituality keeps us in touch with ourselves and our reality. It helps us differentiate and also accept what is in our control and what is beyond. Most importantly it empowers us to handle adversities, build resilience. *It is a way of life.* Dr Debanjan Banerjee, consultant geriatric psychiatrist, Kolkata, and Dr R. Srinivasa Murthy, retired psychiatrist, NIMHANS, Bengaluru, reaffirm the above in their recent paper 'Loneliness in Older People: From Analysis to Action'[6] published in *World Social Psychiatry.* Their paper says spirituality is now recognized to be one of the most important factors in coping, resilience, hardiness building, and stress-reduction strategies.

This is not exclusive to Eastern research and beliefs. A path-analysis model study from Portugal showed the mediating effect of spiritual practices between ageing and perceived social connectedness as well as life satisfaction. A pragmatic group-intervention trial in the senior housing communities of the U.S. involved savouring, acceptance, gratitude and engagement in value-based activities to improve resilience and reduce loneliness.

Dr Banerjee elaborates: 'As per our Vedas, there are four ashramas in our life including *Vanaprastha* and *Sanyasa ashramas.* These ashramas in the modern-day context are not about renouncing everything and moving into exile but about self-acceptance and renouncing the resistance and accepting aspects of ageing. Spirituality helps with this acceptance. It aids this growth process.' His paper insists there is an urgent need for systematic examination of the inclusion of spirituality (as outlined in all religions) in interventions targeting loneliness and evaluation of the outcomes.

Vasanti Sundaram, author and actor, experienced this first-hand. Sundaram has been living alone for a few years and has always enjoyed her own company. However, the second wave of COVID-19 turned her world upside down. It impacted her adversely and very deeply. 'I was suddenly experiencing a breakdown. Lack of human touch for over two years—not a single hug, no person to hold my hand hit me really badly. I would cry copiously for no reason at all. Then one day a friend informed me of a daily Bhagavad Gita class that was starting online. I had never sought Bhagavad Gita before and never read it. But this Bhagavad Gita, its eighteen chapters, has transformed my life completely. It has picked me up, held me together, and given me the feeling that I am not alone. I don't need crutches; I don't need external validation. These classes have been integrated into my routine now. It's been eight months—I chant, I read the Bhagavad Gita every day, I listen to discourses. I feel empowered. All those tears, anxieties and insecurities have just vanished. It's not just the reading of Bhagavad Gita or doing the chanting. Again, that's ritual-based, but it's more the wisdom, the learning, the insight, the clarity that suddenly a veil has been lifted from my head, and I can see everything so clearly. So, spirituality, if this is what you call spirituality, has really turned my life around.'

Sundaram may be doing very well now but we wondered if this could happen for everyone and be lasting.

'Spirituality is like an anchor that keeps us grounded and prepares us to handle adversities better. It is not delusional optimism. If one is low and is feeling sad then they should feel the emotion and let it pass. Spirituality lends resilience', Dr Banerjee explains.

Wakhlu reminds us of our in-built emotional guide system. 'The purest form of spirituality is where there is no "I" or doer in the situation. It is just being present in the now and feeling one and whole with the Universe's creation. It's just about PIN (Presence in Now).'

So, spirituality is not about finding escape or turning away from reality and living an illusion that can shatter anytime. It is about changing the way you view life, accepting its ups and downs more willingly and getting better at handling external stimuli and triggers. Being more of an observer of the movie called life rather than playing a very active role in it.

So How Do You Get Started?

Spirituality is like a seed that is present within all of us. With the right nourishment and an enabling environment, it sprouts and grows into a healthy tree with deep roots, making it resilient to storms or external adversities. In the face of a storm, a stem or two may break and there may be some temporary damage but the sturdy roots help it hold its ground and grow back further. Nithya Shanti elaborates: 'So this is the paradox. We are giving you a map to enter the room that you're already in. This is not taking you somewhere else. This is a journey from here to here, actually.'

Introducing some daily self-care practices into your routine can make for a good starting point.

Spiritual practice is a daily cleansing. Negativity must be washed away if we wish to attract positive experiences in our life.

—Sri Anandamayi Ma

We spoke to multiple practitioners and have compiled some *key practices* to get you started.

Gratitude practice: This is a very empowering practice which encourages you to look at things that are going well in your life and feel gratitude for them. It could be something as basic as food on your plate, a roof on your head, clothes on your body to having friends and family, having a mobile body and active mind or even the bed that you sleep on.

Oberoi shares that every morning he makes his own bed. He thanks the bed that gave him a restful sleep and this practice sets a positive tone for his day. Shanti suggests start, end and fill your day with gratitude. Count or write ten things you are grateful for. 'What you focus on expands!'

Meditation: Take a break from all your gadgets and spend some time with yourself daily, allowing yourself to quieten your mind. Become mindful and aware. Focusing on your breath in and out of your nostrils can help you keep the focus. Mind may wander, thoughts may arise. Allow them to. Catch yourself getting distracted and keep bringing back your focus to your breath. You can find many apps like Calm, Headspace, Insight Timer, among others, that offer guided meditations and calming music to meditate on. If not sure about using mobile apps, you can find meditations and music on YouTube as well.

Shanti recommends meditating for a minimum of four minutes a day and ideally a number of minutes as your age. 'Be comfortable in your discomfort, rest in your restlessness. Be clear about your confusion. Be fearless to face your own fears. Go ahead and meet yourselves.' He suggests the Brahma Vihara practice of the Buddhist tradition along with a practice of gratitude. He explains the four Brahma Viharas.

Metta/Maitreyi – Feel loving kindness towards self and others.

Karuna – Practice compassion towards self and others.

Mudita – Find appreciative joy or rejoice in the happiness of others.

Upekkha/Upeksa – Equanimity or keeping a balanced mind.

'Appreciate what is true, good and beautiful and bless what is not yet true, good and beautiful through the four Brahma

Viharas practices. *Pin poth* is an interesting practice in Sri Lanka where they keep a record of all the good deeds one has done in their life. Make a list of things that you did that were kind, generous, skilful or wholesome. This changes your opinion of yourself as we tend to be very hard on ourselves.'

Breathing exercise or Pranayama: Dadashreeji suggests pranayama or breath control. With simple pranayama, one may cleanse the body and mind, aligning subtle energies of the body. It keeps the body–mind unit active and alive to experience life. One may choose any type of pranayama that suits one, but do it at least twice a day.

Self-inquiry: Byron Katie, seventy-eight, a California-based international speaker and author recommends, The Work as the basis of living a happy life. Katie lived a painful life for over a decade, ailing with agoraphobia. 'It was in 1986. One day, as I lay sleeping on the floor, my self-esteem so low, my self-loathing so great, that I didn't believe I deserved a bed to sleep in. So, even with my bed in the room, I was still sleeping on the floor. This cockroach crawled over my foot and I opened my eyes. In that moment I saw how suffering was born and I saw how to end it. I realized it was a state of mind. When I believed my thoughts, I suffered and when I didn't believe them, I didn't suffer. This is true for every human being. That's where inquiry, what I call The Work, was born.' The Work is a self-inquiry method based on four questions that can help change your outlook on any distressing situation in your life. She suggests stilling your mind and noticing who or what is upsetting you and why. Witness the situation. Find the reason you were upset. Write down your stressful thoughts in simple short sentences, without censoring yourself. Then isolate one thought and use the following set of questions to navigate your way to the answers. The inquiry method allows you to separate the real truth from the made-up truth of a situation.

The Four Questions

Q1. Is it true? Answer either yes or no, honestly. If your answer is yes, move to question two. If it's no then move to question three.

Q2. Can you absolutely know that it's true? Go deeper and introspect if you can really be sure that it's true.

Q3. How do you react, what happens, when you believe that thought? Witness the feelings, body sensations, and behaviours that arise when you believe that thought.

Q4. Who would you be without that thought? Closing your eyes, return to the situation. Take a moment to reflect, observe, and experience the situation again, this time without the thought. Who or what you would be without the thought? How would you see or feel about the other person? Drop all of your judgments. Notice what is revealed.

Finally, you turn around the situation and find opposites of the thought. To do the turnarounds, find opposites of the original statement and evaluate if the opposite is as true as or truer than the original thought.

Often, it's our assumptions about a situation that lead to our misery. Questioning those assumptions through this kind of self-inquiry method releases us from the grip of those debilitating thoughts. In Louise Hay's words 'It's only a thought and a thought can be changed.' Oberoi agrees: 'Life is a manifestation of our thoughts.' Taking ownership of our happiness and finding it in little things around us, drawing inspiration from nature and its grandeur can help us get in touch with our reality. We will continue to encounter bitter or harsh experiences as there is no running away from that. These are an integral part and parcel of our life journey and part of our growth process. But our changed attitude and our spiritual practices can assist us in rebounding faster, climbing out of that ditch sooner. We can all take a cue from Khem Lata Wakhlu, when she says, 'While I suffered through those forty-five days, today when I look back at them, I realize they were instrumental in my growth.'

Dr Sujata Shetty, author of 99 Not Out[7] and a Bhagavad Gita teacher, agrees, 'We will get the knocks in our life. We call them red lights—these terrible things that happen in our life that awaken us from our slumber and act like messages telling us it's time to start working on ourselves. And when you start to work on yourself, even though the external circumstance may not sort itself out but because the internal environment is much cleaner, you are more at peace, and you can problem-solve better. So, your life actually starts to improve as the frequency and intensity of disturbances starts to reduce.'

'Don't look at spirituality as a way to end anything or make you a monk! However, a by-product of it may yield in ending one's pain and suffering. Spirituality simply wants to free you from the bondage of ignorance. And the process of it does not depend on any age', says Maitreyi Dadashreeji.

So, can one expect a completely blissful state or enlightenment at the end of it?

Shekhar Kapur, actor and director, shares an anecdote on his blog[8] that answers our question aptly.

He writes: 'Years and years ago I had trekked to the Rongbuk Monastery, which is the last Monastery on the way to the Everest Base Camp...where I met a young Monk that kept laughing. He must have been in his late twenties at that time, and we spent a lot of time talking. He had been at the Monastery since he was a little boy. I don't remember much of the conversation other than him laughing at my attempts to eat Yak meat that is incredibly tough especially when cooked at those altitudes. But I do remember asking him how long he had been practising meditation.

"15 years," he said. "And how long can you truly be 'in meditation'?", I asked.

"About a minute," he replied as he laughed.

Kapur goes on to reflect on this incident, 'Buddha's Enlightenment did not just happen, I guess. The path to union with the Self is a lifelong journey that involves every step I walk, every breath I breathe, every thought I think and every word I speak. Knowing that not a single moment must be wasted. It is a torturous, tough, devastating and exhilarating journey. And not one amongst us can say for sure what lies at the end of it.'

Shanti says, 'We are all work-in-progress and will always be. Our purpose here is awakening.' Dr Shetty elaborates with an analogy from the Mahabharata: 'Lord Krishna is like our soul, Arjuna our intellect and the Kauravas are all the negative forces, which is why they're larger in number. It's important to understand that it's not easy till we get more disciplined in this spiritual practice. That's why it's so easy to slip, so easy to forget our practices.'

So, can you expect yourself to always be peaceful, unfettered and unruffled? The answer is a definite no. None of us can be that. We will still have days when we are angry or sad. It may take a few days before we can bring ourselves out of these emotional zones and that is perfectly fine. The biggest and most crucial premise of spirituality is being aware and staying connected with the self. Practising self-compassion and being kind to yourself, cutting yourself slack for falling off the horse is our most important dharma. Seeking help and support or cutting yourself from toxic situations is important too.

Through our conversations we also came to understand that spirituality is not inaction or blind faith, hoping and praying for miracles. We still need to take inspired action to deal with the situation we may be in. We may still need to go headlong into some situations for they demand so but our approach, our attitude, our decisions can be more aware and guided through our practices.

Oberoi makes a point with an incident from his life. 'A few years ago, I was acting as a mediator between a moneylender and a family member, helping them resolve a situation. Suddenly like a bolt out of the blue, I was all over the news and falsely accused in a cheque-bounce case filed against me and my family in order to extort money from us. I was raging with anger because my family's name had been maligned. I called up Sister Shivani telling her that I am going to really bring some sense into this person and teach him a lesson. Sister Shivani asked me to send him love, pray for his happiness and to meditate. I was aghast. How could I do that for someone who was hurting me and my family! However, under her guidance, I tried and I tried really hard. It wasn't easy but then I also didn't resort to violence. I filed a defamation case against him and filed an FIR with the police. I took action that was necessary to protect myself and my family. Slowly the person and the situation faded away from our experience.'

'A spiritual lifestyle navigates you towards truth, freedom, peace, harmony and love. While it does, you automatically move away from the pain, disharmony, hate and fear. We invite illness due to these negative elements. By embracing positive spiritual values, your body and mind both, start working at a higher peaceful vibration. Remember, it is a process. So, every now and then, one will experience change within; old pain will emerge with a purpose of dissolution into freedom. The elevated level of awareness helps you to see a higher reality in every experience you encounter,' says Maitreyi Dadashreeji.

Can Spirituality Help Us Age Better?

Shanti has a unique take on this. 'As you grow older your senses decline. Is that a bad thing?' he asks, before sharing, 'I think it's a good thing. The fact that you can't read so much, you can't hear so well or you can't taste so well is nature's way to turn down the settings and give you one last chance to look inside. So, if you didn't do it your whole life then please do it now. Everything is a gift. It's all designed for your awakening.'

Tom Verghese, Melbourne-based cultural coach and author, calls the sixties a transition phase that people need to prepare for. 'Ageing is a transition that is inevitable in life and we can either move through it unconsciously or we can engage with it thoughtfully and be conscious.'

In Sikhism, *chardi kala* refers to a positive attitude or approach to life where *chardi* in Punjabi means rising or soaring and *kala,* a word of Sanskrit origin, means energy. So, chardi kala would mean a highly energized, ever-soaring state of the spirit of an individual. It is characterized by faith, cheerfulness, optimism, discipline and fortitude to do what's needed even in the face of life's difficult challenges. At the core of chardi kala is an acceptance and belief that everything happens for a reason.

Khem Lata Wakhlu's indomitable spirit says, 'Age is just a number, the number of springs, autumns and winters witnessed. If your mind, heart and body are alert it's ok and even if they slow down, it's ok. Ageing is growing, it's a natural process like how a tree grows, flowers blossom into fruits, the fruit grows and, in the end, either it is plucked or it drops off. The fruit doesn't worry about its age. I am eighty-four and I feel all of eighty-four as I have no stigma in my mind. There is no pretence or comparison. I am what I am. As long as I am enjoying each day of my life and going with the flow, I am spiritual.'

Perhaps we can find that acceptance in the poet Harivansh Rai Bachchan's words '*Mann ka ho to achha, naa ho to aur bhi achha*' i.e., 'If you get what you wish for it's great, if you don't get what you wish for it's even better.'

5

Master-A-Second-Innings Stories: How It Can Add Life to Your Years

Aging is not 'lost youth' but a new stage of opportunity and strength.

Betty Friedan

Seventy-one-year-old Veena Iyer is scanning her calendar as we speak. It's chock-a-block full with classes she is conducting, webinars she has to attend and training workshops she is part of. Iyer, a former employee of the State Bank of India, is leading an 'ideal retired life', she jokes. 'I didn't want to spend my days being a couch potato. I wanted to do something enriching with my time and to give back to my peers and the society.'

So Iyer did something she had never done before. She learnt to dance and studied to explore movement. At sixty-six, she enrolled for a Diploma in Dance Movement

Therapy at Tata Institute of Social Sciences, Mumbai. Iyer is now a certified dance-movement therapist running her own workshops and continuously training to upgrade her skill.

Iyer never felt the need to 'retire' and put those much-walked boots up. There was a lifetime stretching ahead of her when she officially retired at sixty. She didn't need to 'earn a living' anymore but she didn't want to spend the rest of her life, 'being retired, sitting around the house, doing nothing' either.

At sixty-five, B.S. Amarnath from Bengaluru actively explored the job market for older workers. Finance was one of the main reasons why he was looking for work but there was another compelling drive, much like Iyer's. 'I felt I still had the capacity to work and wanted to use my time.'

Do Iyer and Amarnath sound like you or someone you know? If that 'capacity to work' comes across as familiar to you, as it did to us, it's because we all have heard it many times over.

Who's thinking of retirement? I still feel I have many years left in me.

Retirement isn't the end of life!

I have never had a slowing down phase. Why should I? I've always been doing something or the other!

Please know that I enjoy going to work even at this age (though I may occasionally grumble!). So please don't give me well-meaning advice and tell me it's time to retire.

The fear of dulling the sharp edges of oneself by not having anything to do, the purposefulness of being productive and the joy of achievement is the reason many older adults today do not see the official retirement age as a full stop to their productive capabilities. The retirement age in India is still quite low—fifty-eight to sixty—for most, though this has been recently increased in areas like academics. This is an age when many feel more productive than they ever have, with their skills honed over the years and many family commitments fulfilled. Having a longer lifespan also means people may wish to work further not just to utilize their talent and time but also to boost their retirement corpus.

It's the reason why many older adults work towards creating a second innings. It's a vocation or profession that utilizes a person's skills while giving them satisfaction and purpose. It is considered one of the seven dimensions of the *wellness framework* by the International Council on Active Ageing that forms the base of ageing active and better.[1]

Across the world, there are incredible stories of older adults rocking their second innings or reaching the pinnacle of their profession in their seventies that proves age doesn't dull talent and dreams. 'I cannot believe I am here. How can I win over Glenn Close?' Korean actress Yuh Jung Youn, seventy-four, asked only half-jokingly, while receiving the Best Supporting Actress Oscar for *Minari* from Brad Pitt in May 2021.[2]

The Bangkok episode of *Street Food Asia,* a popular Netflix series, features Jay Fei, a feisty seventy-plus cook.[3] She still works six days a week and has received Michelin stars and restaurant icon awards, all in her seventies. Closer home, Amitabh Bachchan is a second-innings role model, making a comeback with *Kaun Banega Crorepati* at a time when his career in films had stalled.[4] His second outing in the movies has him experimenting with quirky roles, like *Piku, Gulabo Sitabo* and *102 Not Out*, a risk he may not have taken at the peak of his career.

A second innings can have many forms. For some, like ninety-five-year-old entrepreneur Harbhajan Kaur of Chandigarh, it may be a first stab at work! Or it could be a chance to explore a hobby you didn't have the time for earlier. Sometimes, it could be the continuation of a career you had from the beginning because you never really felt your skills had come to a stop. Sometimes it could be signing up for a job because you need the money. For some, it could even be volunteering, a chance to give back towards a social cause.

How Can Work Help with Ageing Blues?

There is usually a rosy picture of retirement painted by television ads with genial retirees in lounge chairs relaxing in their immaculate living rooms. Or there is Robert De Niro charming everyone effortlessly with his wisdom and humour in *The Intern*, a Hollywood comedy-drama about a widowed retiree seamlessly becoming part of the furniture in a next-gen New York start-up.

The reality may not always be that impeccable.

It could also be like the Jack Nicholson classic movie *About Schmidt*, where an unhappy, lonely retiree is lost in an endless stretch of time with nothing to look forward to.

'Retirement may not work out the same way for everybody', says Tanvi Mallya, a neuropsychologist working with senior citizens in Mumbai. 'While some seniors chart out their day and routines beautifully post-retirement, for some, retirement from work translates into lack of routine. For most people, retirement is accompanied by the stress of finances, feelings of being a burden, feelings of loss of agency and sense of purpose, and loneliness that may predispose a person to dementia.'

This is one of the reasons a second innings can be mentally stimulating, bringing a sense of achievement, purpose, connections and overall well-being.

It can also bring a shift in long-held mindsets.

On his first day of work at Hatti Kaapi, a coffee chain in Bengaluru known for employing older adults, Lakshmi Prasad, sixty-seven, remembers wondering what he—a former entrepreneur and MNC employee with significant experience—was doing waiting tables!

Waiting tables on the first day was part of the training for everyone at the coffee chain, Prasad realized later. He says working post-retirement has helped him change his attitude and look at the positive side of life. 'It helped me come out of a depressive state of mind after a failed venture and a very difficult time.' Now he handles customer care and training, often counselling other senior citizens who work at various positions in the company as part of their inclusive policy.

Prasad advocates a second innings for everyone and urges them to strive towards doing well in it. 'It's a wrong notion to think you are old so you don't have ambition,' he asserts, saying it may help bring a change in outlook as it did for him.

Chandigarh's Harbhajan Kaur is proof that ambition isn't exclusive to youth or to those who've had a career. When ninety-year-old Kaur looked back at her largely homebound life, she had only one regret—she had never earned and had nothing much to do at home either. Kaur was famous for her culinary skills and her daughter suggested she start making *barfis* and selling them. After a sell-out first batch, Kaur's hands were full, taking orders at home. Now at ninety-five, Kaur's barfis, pickles and chutneys ship pan-India with the help of her family who've stepped in for spreading the word, packaging and sales. Kaur has long reached her initial goal of earning a living and had to even slow down due to a bout of COVID-19 but is far from complacent. 'She is enthusiastic and wants to do ten other things', says her granddaughter-in-law Supriya. 'She is involved in every aspect of the venture including which video was taken for our Instagram posts, which part of India was an order placed from and exactly how many spoonfuls of oil should a pickle jar have on top of it.'

If that is not ambition, a drive to excel and do more, what is?

How Easy Is It to Kick-Start Your Second Innings?

'Most of the people in this newsroom are in their twenties and thirties. How do you think you're going to be able to fit in?' an employer asked Nishi Malhotra, sixty-two, when she applied for a senior position with a media firm. Malhotra, a veteran editor from Noida, went on to work successfully with other organizations that had younger teams but says the bias she encountered against age is real. She has faced it a few times in her career as she grew older, including facing prejudice because of her grey hair on one account, despite a stellar resume.

Malhotra's experience is not rare or specific to India. Globally, employers often use 'coded language' in their vacancy advertisements to filter out older adults. A 2019 BBC report says how the terms used are often 'recent college graduates' or 'digital natives,' a smart way to weed out an older generation because the company wants to appear young and hip![5]

Ageism is often the elephant in the room when hiring decisions are made, trumping other factors like experience and talent. The reality hits hard when you hear the number of attendees at the annual job fair conducted by the Nightingales Medical Trust (NMT) in Bengaluru. NMT runs Jobs 60+, an initiative to upskill and equip senior citizens for a second innings. In 2017, we visited their annual fair at a school ground in Bengaluru. The long line of senior applicants (2000 plus, we heard later) we saw there was an eye-opener for us. Many of them were in their late sixties and early seventies, scanning the few stalls put up by prospective employers and submitting resumes that sometimes had way more experience than the job on offer needed. The number of employers at the fair? Sixty-one.

The last job fair by NMT was held before the pandemic in 2019. Word had spread about the fair and the attendees numbered 5,000—many travelling from cities outside Bengaluru to attend the fair. Swati Bhandari, associate director, NMT, says it's a sign that there is an increased and urgent need for financial independence and continued productivity among Indian elders.

Unfortunately, jobs are few and far between. The number of employers at the NMT Job Fairs has remained between sixty to 100. There's also scepticism among some employers about hiring senior citizens, mainly because of a mismatch in their skills and the roles and requirements of today's organizations. Technical knowledge and remote working still remain alien to many older adults. Work from home, a pandemic-created need, is a concept that many older job seekers find hard to adjust to says Puja Kohli who runs Unfold, an HR consultancy that has been doing a second-innings transition programme for older adults. Both Kohli and Bhandari tell us that jobs requiring a physical presence often present problems like longer commutes and inflexible hours, sometimes difficult for an older person to manage.

Why Are Older Adults Seeking a Second Innings?

If we look around us, it isn't hard to find older adults trying to figure out how to spend their day without feeling lonely or bored. Most of us also come across older family and friends worried about an impending surgery because of the cost involved or stretching the monthly budget because of sudden expenses.

People want to work for multiple reasons: to earn money is the most important one but they also want to feel self-empowered, find purpose in the older years and believe that they are capable. For some like Sandhya Kunjur, who moved on to consulting from a fast-paced job in the hospitality industry, it was a way of 'easing into the retirement mode'. Looking back, Kunjur thinks it was important for her, a once-busy career woman, to transition to an easier and slower pace of life as a consultant. It helped acclimatize her to having more time at her disposal and gave her the freedom to select activities like volunteering and social engagements she could explore alongside.

When she moved from Bengaluru to Mumbai to pursue a new inning as a model and actor, something she had wanted to do since childhood, there were enough naysayers who doubted Kalpana Rao. 'How could you leave your family behind and start acting at this age?' she heard. Rao was fifty-five. The 'family' she was leaving behind was actually supporting her at every step, encouraging her to go and give her love and passion for being in front of the camera a try at the hub of it all—Mumbai. Undeterred by the naysayers, Rao, who had battled sciatica, lost a once-successful business and had gone through depression, moved to Mumbai and put in hard work and love into pursuing what she felt would give her a new purpose. She practised how to take the right photographs, found out where to go for auditions and learnt the ropes entirely on her own. If you are focused on something, then work towards it, despite what people say and don't ever think of age, asserts Rao, who now has several ad films and even roles in films with Shah Rukh Khan and Rajinikanth behind her. Rao thinks it's best to be age-agnostic when you are relaunching yourself professionally, even if it is a second career for you. 'If you want equal chances as younger people then you need to behave equally and not expect any special privilege because of your age.'

Vasanti Sundaram, sixty-three, had always faced the camera as a former television anchor in Dubai. She loved to act and decided to pursue theatre actively as she grew older, despite it being a close-knit circle for a newcomer to break into. She started to work at it consciously, attending plays, signing up for workshops and slowly cultivating her way around the theatre world until she was cast in a play.

The day we meet Sundaram, she is prepping for an audition for a film starring a popular female actor. As we wish her luck, she says how being selected is not as important as the fun she has in the process of auditioning. 'I have so much fun just dressing up for the role and auditioning. I challenge myself according to the brief sent, learn the techniques of the camera, the angles, how I can emote. That itself is a whole journey and I love that more.'

Sundaram says it helps that she is not looking at her second innings as a career. 'I am doing it to keep myself purposefully engaged, so I don't get stressed over the fact that I'm not getting roles despite doing so many auditions.'

But what if the purpose wasn't the only need you had? What if you also needed the assurance of a steady income? What then were the steps you needed to keep in mind? At Silver Talkies we often get emails from senior citizens that reflect the desire to stay occupied and affirm that just like Kaur at ninety, these older adults do not see age as a limitation to their work and ambition:

'I am aged 70 and did teacher training certification. Due to family commitments, I couldn't take up a job. Now after finishing all my family commitments, I would love to start a career…,' goes one of the emails.

Yet another, hints at an interest in a different career after retirement: *'I have retired as a senior manager in the bank. I am a law graduate and interested to start as an advocate in civil and criminal cases.'*

Most older adults registering at Jobs 60+ are from the middle-income group and retired from the industrial sector. Senior citizens are in demand for roles that require supervision and a certain amount of trust and responsibility, qualities we readily associate them with. Facility managers with apartments and institutions, supervisory roles and accounting jobs in small establishments are the most common. Retirees are often considered an asset for smaller companies as they are flexible about compensation but salaries remain an area for improvement. When we ask around among senior citizens and job providers, we find that the pay ranges from Rs 10,000 to Rs 50,000, not always comparable with experience.

When he started sending his resume out to prospective employers, Amarnath was advised to lower his salary expectation by half. At first, he bristled at the suggestion that seemed to make a mockery of his vast experience. But he recalibrated his mindset soon because he saw the limitations of the senior job market and the benefits of regular work that went beyond just the money. 'I knew I needed to be adaptable if I wanted to keep active and positive.' The income is lower than he would've liked but it's money and it helps.

Is There a Senior-Job Market in India?

For starters, it does not formally exist. Kohli thinks generational diversity needs to become an institutional agenda, like gender, disability and LGBTQ are, for better roles, salaries and the formalizing of a senior-job market. While that is the thought she started with, the recent years have brought in unexpected new changes. As workforces grow younger in New Age industries like technology and people start peaking at forty-five, Kohli meets more younger people who are ready to call it quits and are seeking a 'second career' that allows them to do what they love at their own pace. She explains why this trend may create further challenges for senior citizens who wish to look for work.

'Most of the early-retiree talent pool in their forties have an aptitude towards technology so if an organization has to pick and choose among people between the ages of forty-five to fifty-five, where the expectation, the training and the integration is not going to be that much of a challenge compared to somebody in their sixties, they'll go for the younger lot.' In comparison, most older adults seeking jobs are from traditional industries and hence not fully conversant with tech requirements.

Small and medium enterprises (SMEs) are open to hiring older adults but there are unlikely to offer flexible hours or great pay.[6] And many older adults who wish to work to put their capability to use aren't ready to compromise on it. 'I have had salaries of Rs 40,000 to Rs 50,000 offered where retirees from senior positions have said it's not adequate for them', Kohli adds.

The mismatch in expectation and the sad reality leads to a higher attrition rate, deepening the scepticism towards older employees. Given that we are a country with an unemployment rate of 22 per cent among youth, older adults aren't always top priority for employers.

It's not India's problem alone. A 2018 report by the US non-profit AARP, which works with retirees, found that 61 per cent of the older workers had seen or experienced age discrimination.[7]

Enabling Your Second Stripes

There is no set formula to how to go about establishing your second innings except the need for energy, hard work, a certain amount of drive, training yourself if the work requires, projecting the skills you bring to the table and being upfront about it.

Be upfront: In 2017, actor Neena Gupta made headlines when she shared an Instagram post in her now-trademark style: *I live in Mumbai and working am a good actor looking fr good parts to play*[8] (sic). You could call it the understatement of the year given that Gupta is a National Award-winning actress but she had hit a lull career-wise and chose to be proactive. Given the string of performances she has given us since that post, being upfront completely worked in Gupta's favour.

Being upfront about his skills also works for Ramesh Sood, sixty-two, a corporate coach, certified NLP master practitioner and as he is popularly known in the co-working space he frequents—LinkedIn star. When he set about trying to chart a second career path as a corporate trainer, Sood—who had worked in human resources all his life—started sharing his slice-of-life thoughts on LinkedIn. His posts garnered him almost 30,000 followers on LinkedIn, besides getting him speaking engagements and work opportunities.

It's hard to talk to Sood without being interrupted in the café of the co-work space he frequents in Pune. He seems to know everyone—from the office boy in charge of the pantry to the CEO of a start-up stationed there. There are frequent high-fives and quick chats and we realize Sood's demeanour and enthusiasm to genuinely know a person doesn't wane, no matter who it is.

'Innovation, an amount of hard work and the ability to be open-minded and collaborative is the key to a successful second innings,' Sood tells us over coffee. When he realized the power of LinkedIn, he trained himself in how to use it smartly and now spends considerable time building his brand on it. He is on a constant learning path, attending seminars and workshops on coaching and other subjects relevant to his work.

Upskilling works: Upskilling is a necessity for retirees getting back into the workforce, starting with basic computer skills such as MS Office or Tally to upgrading specific skill sets like training and coaching certifications, human resource skills, language classes or any course that can help your prospects. Amarnath now works with Bengaluru Allergy Centre. A mechanical engineer by training, he took courses in smartphone training, human resources and upgraded his knowledge of computers. Since he works in a medical environment, he is now teaching himself pharma terminologies, sometimes aided by his doctor son.

Kritarth Malhotra, who co-runs Hum India, an online community-based platform that helps to create job opportunities for seniors, thinks it's especially needed for retirees getting back into the workforce. Malhotra's start-up has done upskilling programs with retired bankers, among others. 'In some sectors like IT, banking, accounting, manufacturing, management, HR, upskilling can be beneficial', he says. 'Seniors need to have the right communication about what they will gain out of it to get them interested.'

Upgrading tech skills is the need of the hour even if you wish to progress in a job you've held for half your life. The once tech-averse Lalitha Desikan, principal of Vidya Niketan school in Bengaluru, rejigged her technical skills in her late sixties when smartboards were introduced in classrooms. The other challenge came when the pandemic struck and learning went remote. 'If I hadn't equipped myself with these necessary skills, I might have had to retire from the very satisfying job that I have. In order to stay relevant at work, I had to change my thinking towards technology.' Like Desikan shows, an open-minded attitude matters everywhere and a long-standing career is no exception.

Bridge the generation gap: Intergenerational encouragement from family or friends could go a long way in helping an older adult soar. Kaur couldn't have achieved her dreams to the scale she has in her nineties without the support of her family. They helped create a brand for her through Instagram, where she has over 20,000 followers. Despite erratic health issues and a recent bout of COVID-19 that saw her away from the kitchen for a while, she does the recipe formulation, ingredient preparation and supervises quality control. Her forward-looking attitude and keenness to try new ideas make the family come together and help her out.

New learnings: Is it prudent to start a second innings in a new area? We feel somewhat silly as we throw the question around among our older friends. One of them moved to study counselling after a media career. Another decided to complete her PhD. Institutions across India now offer lifelong learning courses. It's a great opportunity to explore a whole new world that might become your new career. Mala Honatti, sixty-seven, enrolled for a master's degree in yoga from Shoolini University in Solan, Himachal Pradesh. Over a patchy network, Honatti, a former banker, tells us how much she loves living in the hills as she continues her course and her lifelong fascination for the outdoors. Honatti has been a podium finisher in many Masters Athletics events in India and frequently takes older adults on trekking expeditions. Working in a similar industry was a natural fit and she trained with an adventure sports company after early retirement to understand its workings. When she finally decided to turn her passion into a second innings, yoga, a fitness method she felt would work for her and also her clients, was a perfect choice.

As we talk to people across the spectrum, some learning a short course, some completing a thesis, some enrolled in a diploma, some experimenting with camerawork, we discover curiosity, an unending love for knowledge, in some, and the need to come up to speed with today's setting, in others. Not once does age come up as a blocker in these conversations.

The Many Shades of a Second Innings

Whether it's working from a typical office setup, entrepreneurship or a hobby-turned-venture, your second career needn't always follow the route of your first one. Before you start, it is important to think through the following:

- What is the reason behind pursuing a second inning? Is it financial? Is it to have a purpose to your days? A reason to utilize your capabilities?
- Have you mapped your skill with the kind of work that you wish to do?
- If you've worked all your life, is there a niche skill you could market to potential employers?
- Is there a hobby that you could start off as a venture?
- Do you wish to train yourself in a new field and explore it?
- If planning to pursue a business that is capital intensive, do you have the means to fund it or secure a loan?
- Do you have the support of your loved ones? If not, are you ready to stand your ground for what you believe in?

Once you have the clarity, explore the options. Here are some we have culled out.

Volunteering: Your second innings could be about personal growth and fulfilment through volunteering, like Kunjur who set up a non-profit to educate girls. COVID-19 may have stopped on-field volunteering options for some but there are opportunities you could explore from home. At the Silver Talkies Club, some of our members volunteer with Meghshala, an education start-up, helping them translate their lessons into regional languages.

Accounting/Supervision: Many job openings for retirees seem largely in the areas of accountancy, insurance, administrative work and marketing. Some retirees with specialized domain experience have also explored working with firms and start-ups as a mentor/coach.

Content writing: If you have an interest in words, you could give content writing or editing a go. From the ed-tech sector to the beauty business, content writing can seem daunting to break into at first but consistency and perseverance could get you regular paying gigs. Several successful content writers are happy to share their expertise. Explore Facebook groups for content writers where opportunities and tips are often posted and find out what the competitive market rates are, even if you start small.

Translation services: Textbooks that need to be translated, company agreements in a foreign language, translation services are in demand and the list is endless. If you have the skill of knowing different languages, put them to use.

Teaching: You could start by offering tuition at home if you have a good grasp of a subject and have kept up with modern methods of teaching. Having a background in education usually helps with this. If you are comfortable with technology, you could explore options to be a teacher with e-learning forums. If financial reasons are not the driving force, contact organizations that work with children from underprivileged backgrounds who are always in need of teachers.

Modelling and acting: With urban senior citizens becoming a profitable segment for marketers to reach out to, there has been an increase in the demand for senior models and actors. If you are fit, confident, like facing the camera and have the tenacity and perseverance, this could be a second innings worth pursuing.

Hobby turned venture: Jayasree Chakraborty, seventy-five, started a home venture called The Sari Show of hand-painted fabric in her late-fifties, little knowing how that venture would become her wellness lifeline as she grew older. With social media platforms, WhatsApp broadcasts and by participating in small exhibitions, Chakraborty has managed to sustain her business for the past decade and more. You probably have senior entrepreneurs like her in your own backyard—from the aunty bottling mouth-watering pickles to an ace crochet artist. Smartphones now make it easier to spread the word about your venture and give you that much-needed sense of purpose and fulfilment in the later years.

The Benefits of a Second Innings

'What has starting your own venture brought to your life?"

We put this question to Harbhajan Kaur. The conviction of her reply is obvious even across the distance.

'My self-esteem and confidence have grown immensely. Earlier I was just a wife and mother to someone. Now I am Harbhajan Kaur, entrepreneur. That has been more rewarding than financial independence!'

We think back to what Mallya had pointed out—staying productive is good for our well-being and can help us deal with common age-related blues.

Amarnath rides a scooter to work every day. It helps him navigate Bengaluru's traffic easily and reach on time. As we speak to him more, we realize the joy he gets out of work, even if it is taxing at times and all its parameters may not be exactly what he had wished for. 'Working helps divert my mind from everything. It stops me from brooding and thinking about family issues or any psychological pressures. I would recommend it for all senior citizens.'

Gerontologists tell us that staying occupied and independent is important on the road to ageing well. And a second innings is an important marker of that. This is why countries like Japan have been increasing employment of older workers steadily either by raising the retirement age or by re-employing retirees.

In India too, the Ministry of Social Justice and Empowerment is considering a proposal for flexible career models for senior citizens that include upskilling and the adoption of smart work practices. S. Premkumar Raja, the co-founder of Nightingales Medical Trust and part of the proposal working committee, says it also includes a plan to create a nationwide portal and have helplines where older adults could be counselled for job opportunities and training programmes.[9]

Second careers are certainly part of the talk around seniors in India now, even at the governance level, though the real change may take some time to take effect. In her 2021 budget speech, Finance Minister Nirmala Sitharaman mentioned utilizing senior and retired teachers to mentor younger school teachers and educators through online and offline support.[10]

SACRED, the Senior Citizens employment portal started by the ministry on 1 October 2021, allows older adults above sixty years to register on the portal and find work opportunities.[11] As we browse through the available jobs, we see calls for project manager, security supervisors and professors, mostly aimed at short twelve-month engagement. It may not be much at this moment but as Raja notes, it is at least the beginning of acknowledging an important need.

Like Kohli never tires of mentioning, generational diversity needs to become part of the conversation, with employers setting up orientation and counselling centres for their retirees and creating awareness in their respective industry sectors to sensitize people to the idea of a second innings.

Raja adds that another often-suggested idea is to transition older employees in the senior rung into the role of mentors. Many older adults tell us about the elderly guides, cafeteria supervisors, museum attendants they have come across on visits overseas and wonder if such arrangements could be made for interested senior citizens in India to give them an engagement opportunity, even if at a lower compensation.

As government plans and policies around enabling a second innings become part of the talk, one thing is amply clear. As the world changes and our lives and society start doing a 360-degree turn, the conventional definition of retirement is taking a spin. 'What is retirement?' a senior asks us. 'I simply quit my teaching job and started something else I wanted to do. I don't know any other way to live, without doing anything!'

6

All We Need Is Love: Why Companionship Matters

I finally know the difference between pleasing and loving,
obeying and respecting. It has taken me so many years to be okay
with being different, and with being this alive, this intense.

Eve Ensler, I Am an Emotional Creature

Old love is different, writes author Eve Pell in her essay
'The Race Grows Sweeter Near Its Final Lap' in the
famous Modern Love series.[1] Pell's essay is about the few
years of bliss she had with Sam, a widower she met when
he was seventy-seven and she was in her late sixties. 'In
our 70s and 80s, we had been through enough of life's
ups and downs to know who we were, and we had learned
to compromise. We knew something about death because
we had seen loved ones die. The finish line was drawing
closer. Why not have one last blossoming of the heart?'
she writes.

The words sound familiar to Asavari Kulkarni from Pune. When we visit her, she has finished making a snack. 'I enjoy trying out new recipes,' she says, bringing us steaming mugs of tea and poha. Kulkarni lives in a traditional middle-class neighbourhood in Pune. It's the last place we expect to find someone quietly turning tradition on its head.

Kulkarni is seventy and in a live-in relationship with Anil Yardi. They met at Happy Seniors, a companionship group for older adults in the city. When she and Yardi connected, Kulkarni was hesitant but liked the idea of having a companion to share her days with. Yardi, a widower, felt the same. Neither of them wanted marriage, yet they wanted to give their attraction, shared love for travel, movies and theatre a chance. They have been together for seven years now. Her description of what the relationship means to them is much like Pell's. 'I'm glad we met and we took a chance. We have had our ups and downs in life. Who else would I have spent my older years watching a beautiful sunset with?'

Love in Late Life

Late-life companionship is still new in India, though growing in largely hushed numbers. Not everyone is as open about their relationship as Kulkarni and Yardi are. While many older adults are now ready to give companionship and love a chance, despite the hurdles, there is also a bit of hesitation involved.

Is companionship important? Single older adults we speak to don't shy away from saying it is. But, many of them, especially independent older women with varied interests, are also wary of investing time and energy in it. 'I feel that attachment creates pain. Is it worth creating another level of attachment now? You need a companion and that's an emotional need. But then the logical part of the brain says: caution. My logical brain takes over my emotional need,' says author, former television presenter and journalist Vasanti Sundaram from Bengaluru. Sundaram, who's sixty-two, was married for forty years. She is refreshingly honest about the need for companionship and has even tried out dating apps very briefly, encouraged by her children who live overseas. However, at this point in life, Sundaram, who has a fulfilling second innings in theatre, doesn't feel a compelling need to make the effort to meet new people. 'After sixty it needs a lot of work to find the right one. And you keep thinking whether it's really worth your time, as you're happy on your own and by then, used to your singleness.'

M, a businesswoman from Mumbai, is open to finding a companion but shares Sundaram's cautiousness. 'I am not looking for casual sex, marriage or becoming a caregiver to someone, and most men I have come across need one of these three or all. I am looking for a matching of minds and interests. Our views are so hard-set by fifty-five–sixty that it's hard to change that. After leading a life largely on my own terms until now, I'm not ready to make adjustments unless it really is the right person!'

Nellore's P. Rajagopal, sixty-six, found his right person with Indira Naidu, sixty, in 2016. The retired assistant commissioner from the Railway Police Force felt the vacuum of his wife's death keenly as his children were overseas. When he joined a senior citizens group in Hyderabad to meet others his age, he wasn't looking for love. 'My late wife was everything to me but life was very hard without her, especially in the evenings.' But then he met Naidu, who had lost her husband to a heart attack and felt there was a connection worth exploring. When the couple decided to get married, their children supported but Naidu's relatives raised objections. It wasn't appropriate for a woman in her mid-fifties to tie the knot, they said. In their six-year marriage, Naidu and Rajagopal have faced social ostracization but don't regret their decision. After initial hiccups and adjustments, they now have a happy life together with yoga as a common goal.

How to Find a Late-Life Partner

In the Western world, dating in your older years isn't a society-defying, out-of-the-box act. In India, we tend to view the older years with a limited lens that is a mix of reverence, illness and withdrawal. Age is inextricably linked to moral cut-offs that scoff at self-love and desire. Late-life desire, the instinct for companionship and living your life beyond stereotypes, is still eyebrow-raising. Ask yourself how you would react if an older loved one decided to seek a partner. You may be encouraging but the rarity of the idea may make you pause, even if for a bit.

That mindset is seeing a slow-paced change, especially in urban areas. 'I know my mother is seventy and some may laugh at her interest in finding a companion', says Sheena, a social media influencer, 'But she may have twenty years of her life left. What's wrong if she finds someone to share it with?'

According to the Longitudinal Ageing Study report published in January 2021, 3.4 per cent of those above the age of forty-five years live alone.[2] The 2011 Census data says almost 15 million elderly Indians live alone and three-quarters of them are women.[3] A longer life span, breakdown of bigger families, higher disposable incomes and changing social norms means that people now want to make their later years count. One way to do that is to find someone to share it with, despite social censure and, often, lack of opportunities to meet with interesting senior singles.

You are no longer going to college, attending social events teeming with other single people your age or having water-cooler conversations at work. Where then, do you meet someone?

In the last few years, companionship groups to match senior singles have come up in some cities. Pune's Madhav Damle started Happy Seniors after seeing the loneliness and depression many of his single older acquaintances fell into. Started in 2012, Happy Seniors is open to all men and women above fifty. Damle charges Rs 5,000 for men who wish to join but there are no charges for women. 'Because it is a massive step for many older women to even think of approaching us to find a partner', he says. The group does icebreaker events like picnics and road trips. Damle says he has managed to match almost thirty-forty couples through his group, with some opting for marriage and some choosing to stay together.

In Kolkata, Dr Amitava Desarkar runs Thikana Shimla, a non-profit that provides a platform for senior citizens to connect, apart from helping with other eldercare needs. 'Attraction for the opposite sex is natural, even in the twilight age', he says. Desarkar is bold and unapologetic, despite some conservative backlash he has faced. 'Having a relationship and finding companionship with the opposite sex is one of the best solutions for alleviating loneliness and social isolation in older years,' he asserts.

N.M. Rajeswari founded the Hyderabad-based non-profit Thodu Needa in 2010 to provide emotional support to the elderly. She herself has led by example and has been in a live-in relationship. She and her companion also maintain their finances separately to keep the relationship clean and independent.

When she started, Rajeswari worried about the social stigma that a matchmaking service for seniors would bring but tackled it head-on by holding a press conference and doubling it up as her first meet-up. Forty-five men and twenty-five women attended, with a sixty-six-year-old man and a sixty-three-year-old woman meeting there for the first time and deciding to live together.

You have probably heard about Gujarat-based Natubhai Patel's Anubandh Foundation, courtesy the wide press he has received, including an appearance in the Aamir Khan show *Satyamev Jayate*. Patel, who is seventy-one, started it after the devastating Gujarat earthquake of 2001, that left many survivors without a spouse. His foundation reaches out all across society and organizes 'matchmaking *sammelans*'. Given the paucity of women signing up due to social taboos, he even offers them monetary incentives from a potential partner. It may not be everybody's cup of tea but Patel insists that often it works in providing security for women and encourages them to enrol.

Most of these matchmaking organizations work with traditional-minded seniors who wish to follow the conventional route of finding a match, with age being the only irregularity in the mix. The end goal is marriage and, in some cases, live-in relationships.

What happens if you wish to test the waters slowly and just date?

Online dating is your best bet so far. Tech-savvy, urban elders are now exploring dating apps—until now the playground of younger Indian singles. Ravi Mittal of the dating app Quack Quack saw a 30 per cent spike in signups from fifty-plus and above during the pandemic. Most of the fifty-plus users came from metros. What are older singles looking at, we ask him. 'It seems to be varied', says Mittal. 'Most are aiming to kill loneliness with some companionship and chat with people in the same age group. Some are also interested in casual dates.' Mittal thinks ten years down the line, online dating is how most senior singles will meet others in India. At the moment, it is a new landscape for many, with men outnumbering women.

M has explored dating apps while living overseas and in India. She says online dating for older women is a barely-there scenario here. 'I signed up on Bumble before the pandemic, really looking to chat with someone interesting or find someone to meet over coffee or dinner. The problem is that most men in my age range seem interested in younger women or are looking for a companion-cum-caregiver. I'm plump and faced some ageism and body shaming. I'm not looking at casual hook-ups but I see no reason to stop being on a dating app because I'm in my fifties.' M hasn't tried any senior citizen companionship groups or matrimonial websites for older adults. She admits that online dating can be frustrating as the apps focus on younger people but thinks senior matchmaking groups cater to a different need. 'Senior groups are certainly providing opportunities but the end goal seems to be marriage, something I'm not keen on anymore.'

What Are People Looking For?

As a social scientist who has researched the urban older adult extensively, Tannishtha Samanta, a Professor of Sociology at FLAME University, Pune, has spoken to many older singles and couples across India. What was 'disheartening' as she researched late-life companionship was the continuity of patriarchal practices she saw among some older women, even if they were taking the bold and unusual step of re-partnering late in life. Most of them took on the role of a caregiver, cooking and keeping house while the man in return gave her a home and the feeling of security. Most men were looking for someone to take care of them, Samanta notes in her study 'Love in the Time of Aging: Sociological Reflections on Marriage, Gender and Intimacy in India'.[4]

Rajeswari says over a decade the expectations at both ends have remained the same. 'Women want someone with money and men mostly want a healthy and beautiful woman who can look after them. Also, now women do not mind a younger partner.' Rajeswari recently matched a sixty-three-year-old doctor with a sixty-five-year-old female friend. Her latest client is a fit and active seventy-five-year-old. 'She's looking for a younger person in his seventies as an eighty-year-old may not be mobile or active. If there is a match in the thought process, many women are open to men younger than them too. That's something new I'm seeing now.'

Expectations largely stem from our social conditioning. 'Older Indian men are not used to taking care of themselves unless they've been single all their lives. Many older women do not have savings in their name, with family funds controlled first by the husband, and then the son. In that case, they look for someone who will take care of their financial needs later in life', Damle tells us.

Life choices are diverse and some women do not mind the caregiving. Patel puts us in touch with Neeta

Desai, seventy, who is staying with her seventy-one-year-old companion Harish Doshi in Ahmedabad. We had to change their names on request. Desai doesn't mind taking care of Doshi's dietary needs, managing the kitchen and taking care of his health. Doshi is diabetic. Desai knew this but liked his gentle manner and the prospect of having a stable home. Her son lives overseas and though he does help, Desai isn't assured of it always. She lived in a rented apartment and felt she needed a man around, even though she had lived on her own for almost a decade since her husband's death. 'There are so many things that are difficult to do alone. Having someone around is mental strength. I am lucky to have found a good person and home.'

Kulkarni too wanted someone at home, though she insists that for her, finance or loneliness weren't the tipping points. She felt lonely but also says it was manageable given her packed social calendar. 'I have a very active social life but as evening fell, I sometimes felt lonely and worried about my health and safety.' Yardi had taken to drinking after his wife's death, to while away the lonely hours after work. It stopped once he and Kulkarni started living together. Over tea and snacks, they tell us how they ended up taking care of each other, in unexpected ways.

How much does physical intimacy weigh in the picture? It is not an easy question to ask older Indians, though Kulkarni doesn't shy away from it. 'I did explore it too as that is also an important part of staying together.' But like most older women, she insists that companionship seems to be more for the sake of emotional support and well-being than physical needs. But intimacy in the older years is not something to shy away from. In fact, pleasure could be looked at differently and explored when older. Sex is an important element for many men regardless of age, according to people running matchmaking services and older women who have been on dating apps. It remains a key reason why many men think of getting a partner—often much younger than them—after the loss of a spouse or a divorce.

Lata, a middle-school teacher from Pune, is sixty-two and wishes not to reveal her last name. She met her companion three years ago and decided to stay with him after knowing him for ten months. She tells us that intimacy is an important part of her relationship. 'Attraction was essential for me to enter into a relationship again in my late fifties, and I spoke openly to my partner about being intimate.' Lata says intimacy has taken on a different meaning for her in the later years of her life. 'Physical intimacy can even be holding each other and sleeping. It mattered to me that I felt comfortable with him in this area too. Physical intimacy shouldn't be ignored just because we are older,' she says. She is refreshingly candid. 'In my age there may be some problems initially from both our sides due to age-related issues. Lovemaking may not always mean intercourse.' Lata consulted a gynaecologist before starting to live with her partner and says societal taboos that older people shouldn't think of sex are hypocritical.

'We both enjoy physical touch and continue to explore it in different ways.'

What It Takes to Make a Life Together at Sixty

A few days before we speak to him, S. Seshadri, sixty-five, who married Suma, fifty-five, in July 2019, was out on an evening stroll with his wife in their apartment in Bengaluru. 'A young lady came up to us and asked us what was the secret to our happy married life. We hold hands and walk, you see,' Seshadri says with a hearty laugh. The happiness of having a partner again to share his life with, is evident throughout our conversation.

As the couple talk to us, their comfort in each other comes across in their body language and shared laughter. 'I'm happy,' says Suma when we ask her to describe her life. Yet the comfort wasn't instant. Suma lost her husband a few years before she met Seshadri on an online matrimonial site. It took much convincing on Seshadri's part and an assurance that they would start as friends and move to a partnership only if both felt comfortable about it, for her to take the relationship forward.

How different is adjusting to a significant other at a point in life when habits and beliefs are set and sometimes hard to change?

Seshadri's first marriage lasted thirty-seven years. 'My late wife had already accepted me with all my flaws and ways of living as it happens when you marry young. But I had to re-adjust to a lot of things as Suma is a different person. Some of these changes have helped me orient myself in a better way. It's similar for her too.'

Early on, the couple decided they had to discuss everything so that they could understand each other better. They had gone through emotional disturbances after the loss of their spouses and were keen that they give this second chance their best. It's an ongoing process, says Seshadri. 'We want to be positive about it as we don't want the bad times to come again.'

Yardi says it took eight months for the 'comfort factor' to set in between him and Kulkarni. Before the pandemic, he worked up to 7 p.m. on weekdays and Kulkarni, a retired LIC employee who is socially active, spent her time visiting friends and doing chores. 'The space we got during the entire day also helped us to settle into the relationship in the initial months. We were apart during the day and waited to share the evenings together', she tells us.

Compatibility can be hard to find with age when habits, schedules and choices are well-set over the years. It's also the reason why some matches don't work out in the long run despite the initial high. 'If you think about it, marriage in late life is not much different than marriage in youth', Rajagopal says, 'In both cases, for it to succeed, you need to make some adjustments and get into it for the right reasons.'

The Downsides

Does finding a partner solve everything? Not always is what we find. The before and after of many companionship stories are not smooth sailing, with hindrances along the way or after.

One of the biggest hurdles remain children and social disapproval. Companionship organizers tell us there are growing instances of children coming to meet them with a request to find a match for a lonely parent. But many are also against a parent getting hitched for reasons that vary from property worries to exclusion from a parent's will, fear of losing their emotional connection with a parent and perhaps an inability to see the parent as a human being with normal needs. Often, children can even turn into moral police. 'I'm here against my children's wishes', admits a fifty-three-year-old we meet through Damle's organization. 'They think I'm only thinking of myself and won't be available for them if I find someone.'

A recent Marathi film *Jivan Sandhya* explores the life of two widowed people Jivan and Sandhya who find love in their sixties and want to spend life together to find companionship and care. They believe devotion towards each other is the foundation of their relationship. They get married against the wishes of their children, resulting in ostracization as their children are embarrassed by the parent getting married at an older age. Five years later Jivan's medical emergency forces Sandhya to walk out of the relationship as Jivan's son is unwilling to help out unless this condition is met. The story goes into an emotional roller coaster depicting the sacrifice by the two older adults for the sake of their children, while pining and longing for each other's company. The son understands and accepts their relationship when it's too late. While the movie may seem a little melodramatic to some, it's not too far from reality when it comes to acceptance of new relationships of one's own parents. Emotions are riddled with many thoughts of embarrassment, social stigma and financial concerns, amongst others.

Older people often have property or some wealth they've accumulated over the years, and marriage for them can bring legal complications. It's the reason Damle believes a live-in relationship could be ideal for older couples, provided they can navigate the inevitable social ridicule. 'Often people receive retirement pensions in their deceased spouse's name or a share in the property. The right to those assets may end especially when a woman remarries, so staying together may be better.'

Of course, awareness about legal safeguards whether in a marriage or live-in relationship is a must for anyone, old or young.

Sometimes, it's hard to let go of mom or dad enough to share them with another person. The most honest admission to this comes from Supraja, Suma's daughter. 'I was angry when my mother told me about her interest in finding someone. I thought, wasn't I enough? I was very close to my late dad and thought she had forgotten him.' It also made her more mindful about spending time with her mother. As the two grew closer and once Supraja found a partner of her own, she understood her mother's loneliness and encouraged her to re-partner. In fact, on Suma's wedding day, it was Supraja who comforted and strengthened her mother to go through the ceremony. 'Dad is blessing us. Don't worry, everything will work out, I told her.'

Staying Safe When Finding a Match

Companionships can often result in disappointments and even turn into con jobs. We hear incidents of men blackmailed for money by women or women dumped by men constantly on the lookout for new and younger partners. Sometimes there are court cases that drag on for years. It's the reason many companionship groups put in as many checkpoints as they can at entry.

Rajeswari says a lawyer is present for all couple meetings of Thodu Needa. She also encourages couples to keep her updated with their relationship progress, though few do. Once a couple has met through his group, Damle insists on a notarized agreement, spelling out everything from cooking responsibilities to financial divisions. He asks them to make a will if they haven't and even note down sexual expectations, to avoid any future complications.

Mittal advises caution when meeting someone through a dating app or a matrimonial site. 'People can get easily fooled by financial scams and blackmail.' His advice is to interact a lot over chat to figure the person out and always remember that people often lie online about their age and marital status. 'When you decide to meet up, please go to a public place, where there are a lot of people around. And even if you may not want to spread the word around, always keep a close friend or relative informed that you are meeting someone.'

Human nature is unpredictable and matchmakers mention seeing some couples fall apart after a few months or years, often unable to adjust to another person's lifestyle or demands that were not articulated before. A late-life relationship can be as unstable as one in the younger years. Rajeswari says a practical view helps. 'It's good that people are coming forward to meet others, or their children are supporting them. But it doesn't mean every match lasts long or inevitably leads to happiness, whether a marriage or live-in companionship. People need to be patient and not jump in blindly.'

When Companionship Isn't Just Love

Does companionship always mean a romantic relationship? Perhaps not. Many older women we speak to, tell us how complete their lives are, with work, hobbies and great friendships. Is it enough to have a set of people in your life with whom you can spend time, share things with and on whom you can depend in case of an emergency? Connections that may not have labels but are strong and deep enough to grow old with?

Our friend, Nishi Malhotra, sixty, would say it is worth a try and that there is value in building a network of supportive friends around yourself. In 2017, Malhotra started the group called Just Older Youth, or JOY.[5] It started as a Facebook group for single people aged fifty-five and more. Malhotra, who's single, had just moved to India after several years in the US. Loneliness was one of the reasons behind her move to India. She saw loneliness here too, a disintegrating joint family system, and the lack of a supportive infrastructure for older people. JOY was born out of that idea, and has grown beyond 100 members, over the years. The purpose of JOY is to find living spaces in communities across India (read more about the concept in our chapter 'Ageing in Place'), where members could buy or rent properties together in senior living communities and regular housing societies, to be in close physical proximity and offer support and companionship to each other.

The very idea behind an initiative like JOY is not just the need to find a place to retire in but also the hope that there can be support beyond the traditional norms of a family or a marriage, that there can be support in like-mindedness and shared goals. JOY is a mixed-gender group and Malhotra mentions how both genders can bring support in different ways to the table.

Malhotra makes it absolutely clear to potential members that JOY is not a dating group. What she has observed over the years are the friendships that have emerged from it, especially strong female friendships. Her observation echoes with older single women who often say they value the sisterhood around them. 'Women who are over fifty-five years are no longer really looking for anybody. They have gotten comfortable with themselves and they're enjoying their friends. I feel men still find it difficult to be alone and many are looking for a partner', says Malhotra. 'But older women often find companionship and sisterhood in each other.'

Ideas like JOY may seem idealistic but are needed in a changing world, given that you retain your independence yet are assured of support through very practical means. Malhotra's hope for the future is that with initiatives like JOY, single older adults don't have to face the prospect of lonely and unsupported old age. And more importantly, find options beyond re-partnering.

It's wonderful if you find the joyful love Eve Pell discovered in her late sixties or the easy companionship that Kulkarni and Yardi share. But there should always be options for support and connections beyond it.

7

Social Networks: The Wellness Secret Sauce

The afternoon knows what the morning never suspected.

Robert Frost

In November 2020, our club member Kanchana Arni, sixty, was rehearsing for a play she was performing with some friends for a virtual celebration. On the day of the performance, on a complete whim, Arni went and picked up marigold flowers and made a crown to wear in her hair. She posed for photographs, glowing and resplendent in her bright and gorgeous new look. It's not something she would have done earlier, she tells us. Something about the opportunity, the freedom that comes with age, and being part of a group where she got a chance to express herself, came together to make her experiment. 'It gave me a chance to be wild', laughs Arni, who says she is enjoying her 'senior years' thoroughly.

Arni, who lives in Bengaluru, has often worried over loneliness and the absence of social connections in her older years. Both her mother and mother-in-law craved meaningful interactions and people around them as they grew older. While her mother-in-law succumbed to Alzheimer's disease, Arni's mother grew increasingly dependent on her for emotional support. Arni is an author who has conceptualised books on Indian folk art and has led the travelling life of a diplomat's wife. When she moved to Bengaluru, a city where she had no friends, she consciously worked towards building friendships. She joined groups for older adults and found not just avenues to explore a different side of her but also a new set of friends. 'Being part of a group also keeps me engaged, feeling alive and having fun at the same time', she tells us.

If finding friends and having shared interests gave Arni things to do, it gave Samuel Tavamani, seventy, a reason to live.

'Being part of a group helped me come out of a shell', Tavamani told us recently. He is a member of Silver Talkies Club. When he joined some time back, Col Tavamani, a widower, was one of the quieter members. Recently, over a Zoom call with our members during the lockdown, he shared his adventures in the kitchen. Gone was the earlier reticence. 'I had withdrawn into a shell after the sudden death of my wife because of my grief. This club and my group of army buddies have helped me come out of a self-imposed exile and in the process meet some beautiful and well-meaning people', he says. His story tells us that we all have a basic need to communicate and share, even the most introverts among us. Social connections, interactions and friendships lead to engagement—essential to an older adult's emotional well-being and health. The Greek philosopher Aristotle had said: Man is by nature a social animal. Col Tavamani would tell everyone who cared to listen that he was right.

The Social Engagement Concept

When she founded Dignity Foundation twenty-six years ago and started the conversation around active ageing in India, Sheilu Srinivasan says one of her key focus areas was emotional well-being. 'We paid attention to and engineered activities that promoted this aspect of wellbeing.' To do that, Srinivasan didn't just put a bunch of older adults together. Instead, she created a structure in the groups and their programmes, through Dignity Foundation's Loneliness Mitigation centres. 'Also known as "chai masti" centres, these are a space for senior citizens to meet, build their support networks and lead an active life', she tells us. A path-breaker for bringing social engagement into the ageing conversation, Srinivasan discovered that camaraderie and trusting companionships in the later years were one of the key needs of the elderly. 'Our fifty centres all over the country attest to that need for daily bonding and social connectedness', she tells us.

Globally, traditional communities have often had that daily bonding built into their culture. You may have read about Japan's Ogimi village in the Okinawa prefecture, better known as the village of centenarians. While genetics and diet play a role in the residents' longevity, what makes them poster people for active ageing is the social mechanism of the island. Residents are part of varied interest groups called *moai*, which help them develop emotional connections over shared interests.

In South Korea, *colatecs* or daytime discos thrived for senior citizens in pre-Covid days.[1] They were cheaply priced and allowed older adults to meet and dance with other seniors to escape being lonely.

Our friend Sandhya Rajayer often shares the story of a small temple down the corner from her home in an old Bengaluru neighbourhood. In the early evenings, that's where elderly women in the neighbourhood gather. They sing devotional songs, make floral garlands for the deity and chat about their day. 'That is the traditional concept of ageing healthy', says Rajayer, who rues that such spaces are fast disappearing in our urban neighbourhoods, alienating elders. 'Even new gated communities should have a gathering space where people can come and chat, even if it is only about their day or what their grandchildren did. That is enough for us to feel we have touched another human life.' Rajayer feels such interactions are cornerstones for well-being as one ages.

The unfortunate bit is our urban sprawl is taking away these spaces to congregate, isolating older adults to a great extent. What is replacing these organic gathering spaces are senior groups and clubs instead, both online and face to face, giving older adults a chance for that much-needed social engagement.

So, what is social engagement? The dictionary definition is the level of a person's connectivity to the community around her or him. It also refers to the depth of their interaction with others and how it adds to their quality of life. Often, being part of a group and hearing and seeing others try out things can lead to people discovering an unexpected side to themselves, as Arni did, fuelled by the peer-led enthusiasm and encouragement. It is this reason why social engagement is considered the secret sauce for healthy and active ageing.

The Importance of Engagement

You may wonder about the focus on the need for social connections as one grows older, in this book. After all, isn't friendship usually associated with youth?

Education management expert Ravi Acharya would say no to that. After spending his working years in Pune and Ahmedabad, among other places, Acharya moved to Bengaluru. He is lucky to have two of his closest friends live on the same street. Acharya says we don't realize the importance of actually talking to our friends, in a world dominated by conversations on WhatsApp, Facebook and other social media. 'We friends make it a point to meet once a month', says Acharya, 'and avoid conversations over WhatsApp unless necessary. Such social connections and making an effort toward being in touch is important for active ageing.'

When we ask Chandrika Desai how she stays connected to people, she has a hearty laugh. 'It's my personality,' she says. Desai is a jovial seventy-four-year-old who epitomizes how important social engagement could be. But like she tells us, passively becoming part of a group is not the only way to do it. You need to be active at your end, too. Every morning, Desai sits with a list. She has a large network of family and friends, and each morning she calls different people. 'I make an effort to reach out', says Desai who lives on her own, leads her own life but is deeply connected to her two children who live overseas.

Desai is also part of a group of cousins and friends who meet for lunch every Sunday and have been doing so for years. There is no dearth of friendships and connections in her life but like Acharya, Desai says it is important to maintain that village of friends as one grows older. 'I open up to my friends if there is a need and they also reach out to me. I believe it is important.'

The associations and regular communication help Desai not just find a tribe around her but also a give-and-take-of-support that keeps her life secure and enriched within the circle of friends around her.

'While old friendships are important, it's very exciting to have new friendships too, especially when you connect over shared interests', says Arni. She is currently enjoying gardening, among other things, with a group of friends. 'I never could grow one single plant and now gardening has become a great interest. This constant information exchange, sharing and experimenting is a wonderful way to stay engaged.'

In his book *Being Mortal*, Atul Gawande writes about a programme called Eden Alternative in Chase Memorial Nursing Home, USA. Geriatrician Bill Thomas took over the nursing home and realized what plagued the residents more than their ailments were boredom, loneliness and helplessness. So, he introduced a pioneering idea and brought in animals, plants and children into the mix. The place doubled as a day-care centre for children of the staff and introduced art workshops, and many residents took on the responsibility of caring for the pets and plants! It created a caring, inclusive and vibrant community that improved well-being and is now a model applied both to eldercare communities and for seniors who wish to age in place, that is continue to live in their homes.[2]

You may wonder why we are including this example here. Because this unusual experiment shows what wellness experts have been saying all along—a sense of purpose, which the seniors at the nursing home got from being part of pet care and gardening. An inclusive, vibrant community and connections that can enhance social engagement and improve well-being.

The Need for Connections

There is no denying the life-altering impact of meaningful connections.

It's what US Surgeon General Vivek Murthy explores in *Together: The Healing Power of Human Connections.* Murthy writes how medicine often misses out on this aspect, given that 'social issues, as wrenching as they were, seemed outside the domain of doctoring.' He mentions Dr Julianne Holt-Lunstad's study on the power of social relationships.[3] While pursuing a PhD in Health and Social Psychology, Holt-Lunstad tried to find the answer to the question, do social relationships reduce our risk of dying early? Her study published in July 2010 showed that people with strong social relationships are 50 per cent less likely to die prematurely than people with weak social relationships. The impact of poor social connection on reducing lifespan is equal to the risk of smoking fifteen cigarettes a day, and a risk that's greater than the risk of obesity, excess alcohol and lack of exercise.

Did that data make you go wide-eyed and pick up the phone to call an old friend? Or convince your mother to stop making the TV her best friend and step out to meet her neighbourhood buddies?

Our families are nuclear now, especially in urban areas. Many older adults like Col Tavamani have no one to turn to or converse with when the children are at work or live elsewhere. Some elders may have fewer social connections than earlier. As people retire, they lose friendships and relationships to illness and death. Daily social contacts and stimulations lessen, often impacting their physical and mental health. Other reasons for loneliness include little or no interaction with family members, neighbours or the community at large. The pandemic may have brought that loneliness into sharper focus but it has always been there in our society.

If you have an older loved one, think about what we ask them the most? We enquire about their health—we ask them if their blood pressure, sugar and cholesterol are under control. If they have aching knees and a bad back. We seldom ask if they are in touch with their network of friends or who they would have chatted with on that day. If you are an offspring reading this, chances are that you never imagined that lack of social connections could hurt your parents more than a physical ailment could. But books like Dr Murthy's and research have shown us that it does. In the introduction to this book, we mentioned a survey in 2018 called Jug Jug Jiyenge that focused on elders and their children who live away from them.[4] The 1,000 senior citizens across urban India surveyed said physical health was a major concern for only 10 per cent of them, 36.4 per cent worried about maintaining their social lives. Their children felt the opposite!

Still not convinced that lack of social engagement could be harmful? We met Dr Prem Narasimhan, consultant geriatrician at Jaslok Hospital, Mumbai, to find out the damage it could do. Dr Narasimhan has spent the better part of 2020 and 2021 in Covid wards in his hospital, consulting his older patients over the phone due to the mandatory social distancing.

'Isolation can lead to severe mental-health challenges including depression,' he tells us. Dr Narasimhan runs the Graceful Ageing clinic for seniors at the hospital, encouraging them to speak to him beyond their physical problems. He says that isolation if ignored for a longer duration can lead to depression and 'even thoughts of suicide.' A supporter of structured social groups, something that Dignity Foundation, Silver Talkies and several entrants in the eldercare industry now provide, Dr Narasimhan advises shared learning through fun interactions. 'When one attends a class or lecture among multiple participants one gets an opportunity to meet people with similar interests. It paves the way to have great acquaintances and purpose', he says.

There is a physical downside to the lack of social connection that we seldom think about. This lesson came as quite the shocker to Seher Kapadia, when her seventy-three-year-old mother lost her neighbour, friend and confidante for over two decades to sudden death. 'They had a ritual of visiting each other every evening with a cup of tea to chat about the day. They would be constantly on WhatsApp and the building intercom phone to talk about recipes, which veggie store charged a better rate and share the details of their lives. When Aunty passed on, suddenly that assured interaction came to an end. Aunty had also been the binding factor for my mother and other elderly ladies, hosting them in her home regularly, which came to a stop. My mother lost weight, grew quieter and started feeling and looking duller than she ever had before.' Kapadia only realized this was the problem much later, after several doctor visits. 'It was surprising how therapeutic that connection had been for my mom.'

When social life dwindles, there is a marked lack of exercise that, aside from its physical effects, can also lead to a lack of interest in life. We get a further understanding of that from Meena Vohra, seventy, a ceramic artist who embodies the term joie de vivre. Vohra started Humjoli, an informal support group for senior citizens in a community park of Jal Vayu Vihar, Noida. Her idea was to support elders living alone through crisis and other emergency needs but Humjoli also morphed into a group for entertainment and fun interactions. According to Vohra, 'It helped many of them step out of their house because now there was a reason to. Getting ready for the get-togethers, walking to the park, interacting, talking, everything helped them feel better!' Vohra says the group's collective enthusiasm was infectious enough to even bring some wheelchair-bound residents out of their homes. Being part of the group changed life for many elderly persons in the neighbourhood, even if Vohra had to convince them to take part. What's more, the members served as an inspiration for each other. 'We had cancer survivors as members, we had an eighty-year-old gentleman who lived alone and did all his work himself, including cooking. Such people could show others how you can overcome things and how active one could be even at a later age.' Though, like most senior groups, the pandemic has made Humjoli interactions virtual now, Vohra thinks what still works like a magic drug for many lonely elders are the constant group interactions, WhatsApp chats and phone calls that Humjoli has brought to their lives.

Everyone likes interaction. Yes, there are some of us who prefer the quietude of our own company to being part of a boisterous group. Some may not wish to always be part of classes or clubs or enjoy social situations. But having a tribe around us, a circle of connection, understanding and engaging conversations is important. And it's always good to know that there are opportunities to find your tribe if you wish to, something that several senior groups provide.

The Social Engagement Science

Many of our members tell us that being part of the Silver Talkies Club has helped them get out of their comfort zones. It could've been an art class for someone who had last held a brush in school or dancing to 'Mera Naam Chin Chin Chu' on stage during a celebration. It's what Pushpa Kamath, seventy-five, did during one of our club anniversary celebrations some years back. 'I had last danced on stage to the same number, fifty-five years ago! The confidence came from within and from this group of well-wishers and friends I have in the group.' In less than a year with the club, she had gone for movies and lunches with her new friends; tried her hand at creating art with mosaic tiles, done chair yoga, played memory games and learnt origami. Kamath lived with her son and daughter-in-law but was alone for most of the day with the family busy at work, a common story in most multi-generation homes. 'Being part of a group changed my life', she told us. 'I met people, took part in activities and it left me with no time to think of my age or any sickness. It made me feel healthier and younger.' Kamath wasn't imagining her sense of well-being. Dr Soumya Hedge, the geriatric psychiatrist we often talk to for guidance when working with older adults, explained why. 'You have to look at social connections from a physical and cognitive point of view. If you are stepping out to visit a seniors' group, it's because there's something different in store for you there that's motivating you. Doing new things by going outside your comfort zone in a non-judgemental environment is a huge advantage from a cognitive point of view!' Hegde often follows the practice of social prescribing. She recommends resources to help her patients form social connections that could be beneficial to their well-being—joining activity groups and clubs for older adults, being one of them.

Social connections are the adaptability factor that enable older adults to find peer support, stay mentally engaged and active, improving their overall wellness quotient. We often see the impact of those connections first-hand with members of our club. Our members have found not just friendships but also guidance from each other for many things, from gardening to nutrition. During the lockdown and strict social distancing, they eagerly waited for the weekly online webinars. It was a chance to meet others and feel the comfort of connections, even if only virtual. And it's not just us saying. Geroscience—the study of how to slow biological ageing[5] to extend healthspan and longevity—thinks so too, and has now acknowledged the importance of factors like social connection for ageing in a better way.

Being part of a social cohort can be empowering, and groups need not always be formal. You could join a book club or a circle of knitting enthusiasts, an intergenerational language class or become part of a trio of seniors who walk together every morning.

Connections can also hold you up through tough times. When her late husband was ill and she had to become his primary caregiver, Desai found a huge source of guidance in another friend she got to know through a social group. This person had been a long-time caregiver to her mother and was extremely knowledgeable about the ailment. For Desai, this help was invaluable, guiding her through the emotionally and physically taxing minefield that caregiving can be.

In the twelve years they have run Maya Care, Manjiri Gokhale Joshi and Abhay Joshi have seen benefits of quality social interactions and emotional well-being first-hand. Volunteers from their organization Maya Care have been helping senior citizens across Indian cities since 2009. Accompanying them on doctor visits, buying groceries, helping with bill payment and other tasks, what Maya Care tries to do is fill in where the family can't.

The emotional engagement that Maya Care has provided has been the highlight for many lonely elders. Many of them would often wait for visits from the volunteers just to have someone to talk to and share their day with.

'The thirst is for emotional support and intellectual stimulation,' says Gokhale Joshi who is never short of examples of impact. One of her favourites is of a wheelchair-bound older person who became withdrawn and stopped stepping out of home after a stroke. He gradually started opening up and stepping out after regular interaction and check-ins.

A similar sense of purpose also drives the phone companionship programme that Maya Care launched during the pandemic. Unable to meet them, volunteers called senior citizens a few times a week for a casual chat, ensuring they had everything they needed. As part of Maya Care's inclusive policy, many of these volunteers are younger persons with disabilities, who often channel the conversations towards career guidance for themselves, giving the older adult they are speaking to a chance to delve into their own experience and wisdom. Gokhale Joshi mentions a retired architect in an Indian city who looked forward to his conversations with the phone volunteer and was even ready to step out and meet him in person, to discuss the area of work he was so passionate about.

The impact of the programme has been immense and the couple has now launched the service in the UK, where they live. As they put it, just taking care of logistics when caring for an elder isn't enough. It's the stimulation and sense of purpose in their life that's the real game changer.

Dr Hegde says there is a link between social engagement and the sense of purpose. 'Social connections go beyond gathering at a park for activities or becoming a member of a seniors' club. Not every older person may have the personality for socializing either. As long as you have a purpose to the day that includes interaction, it's good for your emotional and social well-being.'

Your purpose could be anything that makes you look forward to getting out of bed each morning. If you are a younger person reading this and are in your thirties or forties, chances are that you've made fun of a parent who loves to visit the bank in the age of net banking. But as Dr Hegde notes, going to the bank could be an engagement opportunity too! You have met advocate Shiv Kumar in earlier chapters. This sharp and active septuagenarian runs a law firm. Technology isn't his weak point at all but in pre-pandemic days, he believed in visiting the bank. 'Despite being laughed at and being made fun of, I made physical visits to the bank instead of using net banking. It became another activity and scope for meeting and talking to people', says Kumar. Services like Maya Care bring that interaction and purpose to elders, who, unlike Kumar, can't always create it for themselves.

The Need for Family Support

The onus of well-being is not just on the senior. Families too need to be alert towards the needs of their older loved ones to prevent them from feeling isolated and avoid cognitive decline. Saraswathi Natesan, sixty-four, takes time to open up and talk. But when she does, you realize the change social engagement has brought to her life. Natesan has gone on holidays on her own after she lost her husband six years ago. Going on a holiday overseas with a tour group without her family was a huge step for this homemaker who had led a sheltered life. It's her daughters who encouraged Natesan to take the decision and give it a try, and expand her circle beyond her comfort zone— whether it was a smartphone learning class or joining a club.

To Natesan's credit, she has sailed through the doors her daughters have opened up for her, thanks to her open mind and willingness to learn. Being part of a seniors' club helps her make diverse friends, something she wasn't used to earlier. 'Earlier, I did not have an opportunity to meet people from different backgrounds, being a homemaker. Now I'm happy to explore and meet people. I'm also happy to try out new things to learn and travel.'

Dr Hegde suggests thinking out of the box on how you can build interesting variations in an older adult's routine, even if they do not wish to join structured social activities. Our friend Srirupa often asks her mother, who loves to cook, to try out a new recipe and ingredients and share it on the family WhatsApp chat with accompanying photographs. 'It fulfils many purposes—she is busy looking up a recipe, is honing her smartphone photography skills and the eventual share results in an inevitable conversation with the rest of us.'

Going beyond Social Groups – Ways of Staying Connected

Many of us may not always enjoy social interactions, group travel or becoming part of a seniors' club. What we do need to ensure is the quality of the interactions we have around us and the value it adds to our well-being.

• Adapting to technology is a huge way to harness connections especially after the pandemic changed the way we live and interact. You can use technology to stay connected to the people you love. You can try Skype, FaceTime, Zoom or WhatsApp video calling, as the options are endless. Or take a cue from Vasanti Sundaram, who reads bedtime stories to her granddaughter in Canada a few times a week. Sundaram lives in Bengaluru and technology has helped her stay emotionally connected to her only grandchild who lives oceans away. Sundaram and her granddaughter read stories, paint together and spend an hour doing what an indulgent grandmom and a cherished grandchild would've done face to face. 'She has made me download Roblox (a popular mobile game) and we play that together too. The other day we had a cleaning exercise in her room as she had clothes spread all over!' laughs Sundaram, who credits her granddaughter's mother with facilitating this connection. She herself makes an effort towards sustaining it, by waking up at 4 a.m.

every morning to be able to keep her date with her granddaughter in a different time zone. What does it do for her emotional well-being? 'It transforms my day, and on days we don't talk, I feel something is missing.' In today's distanced world, embracing technology as Sundaram and her family do or like Natesan did by taking classes on smartphone use and getting comfortable on virtual platforms, can also help maintain valuable connections and enhance one's emotional well-being.

- Joining a group wellness class is a great way to focus on your health, stay motivated about exercising and find a wider circle, sometimes intergenerational. It's one of the reasons why Laughter Yoga groups are popular across Indian neighbourhoods, especially among seniors. If you are spiritually inclined, being part of a group can help you experience a different kind of energy and support. Being part of chanting forums, meditation groups, the neighbourhood bhajan group has been a source of both spiritual and social succour for many older adults.

- Get involved with a charity or volunteering work in your local community. It would keep you engaged and connected in a meaningful way and work as a cognitive stimulus. Acharya is part of a Bengaluru-based civic group Malleswaram Social that notifies local authorities about infrastructure issues in their neighbourhood. It has helped him find friendships across generations. It has also added to a sense of purpose and achievement when their advocacy finds success.

- Remember *moai*? Learning something new can help with your *moai* in many ways. First up, you share a common interest with fellow learners and find new connections. After a ballroom dancing workshop we organized in Bengaluru before COVID-19 locked us all in, the senior learners had formed their group to meet for a coffee and catch up on each other's lives. Not only had they found a physical activity they enjoyed, but they had also discovered sustainable friendships.

If reading this feels like a loop around social connections, friendships and a sense of purpose, that's because those are simple but important markers on the road to ageing well. You only need to look at the famous Blue Zones around the world to believe that. Blue Zones—the five regions around the world where people live the longest and healthiest—have been the subject of much research in recent years. Although genetics and diet play a big role in that longevity, three simple factors are common to every Blue Zone in the world.

No prizes for guessing the key ingredients of that cocktail—social activity, a strong sense of purpose and a sense of community!

8

Ageing at Home and
Beyond: Getting Ready

It matters not how long we live but how.

Philip James Bailey

We met Urmila in February 2017 when she attended our fabric recycling workshop. Being a textile enthusiast and an adept seamstress, she took to the ideas discussed in the workshop like fish to water. Urmila has always been super active and a master juggler, managing her many roles as a homemaker, caregiver to her late husband who had dementia, a learner, a do-gooder and also an entrepreneur managing a family business. Urmila's children Devangi and Neel are both settled in the US, allowing her space and time to be on top of things. Once Urmila joined the Silver Talkies Club, we would see her at many events. She made new friends and also invited fellow members home to give them a demonstration of her culinary skills and teach them her health recipes. Being amidst company helped her cope well with the loss of her husband too.

Fast forward to 2020–21. Urmila, seventy-four, adapted to the pandemic very quickly and continued to stay positive and active, albeit online. She took it upon herself to muster resources and help those dealing with the pandemic from the safety of her abode. However, she herself contracted COVID-19 in April 2021. Fortunately, her son Neel was in the country and hurried to Bengaluru to support her. She dealt with the situation courageously and despite the anxiety and stress of hospitalization, returned home victorious. However, post recovery she found herself on tenterhooks as she started experiencing repeated episodes of forgetfulness. It started rattling her and we could witness her stress even in our interactions with her. A visit to a geriatric psychiatrist and a few diagnostic tests later, the family found that there are some vascular changes in her brain that require further study. Her world is suddenly changing, compelling the family to discuss and evaluate their plans for the future as Urmila ages.

Neel and Devangi have been actively involved in their mother's wellness and have been considering various options—whether to relocate Urmila to US to be with them or identify a place which could support her well as she continues to live independently in Bengaluru. The former option comes with its own challenges which we hear very often from other NRI families too—older adults find the foreign locations alien and unaccommodating. Lack of company, dependence on children and an unfamiliar territory can be very daunting and confounding. Top it with uber expensive medical treatment, making this choice a difficult one. So, what options does the family have within the country to make Urmila's life easier and supported?

Unlike some developed countries, the concept of senior living communities is nascent and emerging in India. Until as recently as a year ago, senior living communities have been spoken of as old-age homes for elders who are unable to take care of themselves and have no family to care for them. They were considered a social taboo in multiple contexts. However, the recent pandemic has put a spotlight on this housing option like never before. With an increasing number of seniors becoming empty nesters and living independently, COVID-19 has forced them to recalibrate their requirements and slowly open up to the idea of considering senior living communities as a viable, future solution with a supportive ecosystem. A survey by Antara Senior Care a year ago covering 3,000 seniors across three different cities revealed that as many as 77 per cent of seniors are staying alone.[1] Nuclear families are a reality that have warranted a focus on senior living communities as one of the solutions for the changing needs of a senior.

So, what is a senior living community? Simply put, it is a residential project designed and planned especially for older adults, keeping in mind their ageing needs. These communities come with upgraded senior-friendly infrastructure, resources and facilities including healthcare, food, wellness, housekeeping, social engagement and concierge services.[2] Positioned as 'forever homes' for seniors with a supportive and caring ecosystem in place, these residential communities can either be exclusively for older adults or could be part of a larger community that has a building or two designed for seniors, allowing an intergenerational mix.

The promise of a holistic living experience is very alluring. Uma Raiker moved from Mumbai to Bengaluru last year during the pandemic. She and her husband chose to live in Primus Reflection, a senior living community. She realized the need for more help to take care of her husband who has a chronic back issue and to handle any future medical emergencies. The other nagging thought that influenced her move was: 'What will become of the other when one of us passes away?' Their son lives in the US. The choice of Bengaluru was driven by her need to move to a cosmopolitan city and community, having been born and brought up in Mumbai. She is very happy as she now finds herself surrounded by many new friends and has also found relief from day-to-day household chores that can become increasingly burdensome with age. She uses the cafeteria in the senior living community but also cooks her husband's favourite meals sometimes. 'I bring the food home and season it as per our taste and liking', she guffaws. Having help at hand whenever her husband is dealing with a medical issue has been a big relief for her. 'Recently, my husband complained of angina pain on a Sunday. The doctor on the premises checked him and gave him the necessary medicines, checked on him continuously and he was fine.' She now finds time to participate in activities of her liking, surf the internet, interact with family and friends as many regular chores like cooking, cleaning and grocery shopping have been taken off her plate.

Mohit Nirula, CEO of Columbia Pacific Communities, a leading name in the senior living sector, tells us that it is mostly the women of the house who drive the decision of moving into a senior living community. The common reasons that drive the decision are unmanageable housekeeping tasks, dealing with daily help, cooking, fear of medical emergencies and loneliness. 'We are used to living in an assisted living ecosystem from an early age, with a lot of help available to us. With the pandemic there was a realization that we would like to live in this assisted living space forever', says Nirula. 'The demographics have shifted during the pandemic. Our youngest buyer now is forty-eight and the oldest in the early sixties. This demographic was not available earlier. They thought senior housing was for seniors and not them.' Nirula himself plans to move into one of his own projects in the near future as both his daughters live in London and he would like to continue to stay in India. 'I have standing instructions from my friends that as soon as I book a home, I must inform them so that they can do so too.' This seems to be a rising trend where multiple family members or friends are choosing to move into a retirement community together. Hari Baskaran recently relocated to Bengaluru from Delhi to be closer to his daughter and family. Baskaran's wife suffers from an autoimmune disease that requires immediate attention and quick response time when an episode happens, and this is his primary reason to move into a retirement home so that medical help is available for her. His two sisters-in-law who are widowed have entrusted him with the responsibility of identifying a place where all of them can move in together.

Sandhya Kunjur is single and has been living an independent life in Bengaluru since many years after retiring from her corporate life in Mumbai. She moved to Bengaluru to be closer to her family. She is deeply aware that she cannot depend on her family for her needs in the long-term. She would need to make alternate arrangements for herself, and her choice seems to be moving into a senior living community. She, too, wishes that she has a group of friends to make this move with.

With a similar idea in mind Nishi Malhotra started JOY community a few years ago. It is a group of single seniors from all over the country who have come together with a single-minded objective of assessing community living options for themselves. The thought behind the initiative is to find support, comfort and companionship amongst each other and settle down together in smaller groups. The idea of settling down with known people is comforting. The 107 members of the group have evaluated twenty different projects across the country and shortlisted cities and projects of their choice, which are now in different stages of evaluation.

'We choose our members very carefully. Other than the fact that they must be fifty-five-plus and single, they should be willing to relocate', shares Malhotra. She finds many people back out at the idea of relocation. However, relocation may be inevitable if your choice is moving into a senior living community. Given the nascency of the concept, you may find that options are few and far between. North, south and west India have majority of the projects, concentrated, however, in few select cities. A 2018 industry report by CII revealed that there is a huge gap in the demand and supply of senior living units.[3] The current senior housing demand from the urban and rural sector was estimated to be approximately 2.4 lakh houses and 51.5 K houses respectively, while the supply across thirty-seven senior-living providers across all formats and economic segments was pegged at only 20,000 units. Of these only 53 per cent were operational and the rest were under different stages of development—an over 10x gap.

So, what should you be looking at while evaluating a senior living home for yourself or your parents? Some of the common criteria looked into are:

- **Location:** Proximity to the airport, railway station, city centre, hospitals, shopping areas, etc. Accessibility to transport.
- **Project details:** Size of the project, units, floor plans, wheel-chair accessibility, proportion of private vs. common area, open areas, parking facility, guest facilities, any community restrictions, pet friendliness, etc.

- **Design considerations:** Age-friendly design principles planned in the project—for instance, height of shelves for easy accessibility in kitchen and bedrooms, bathroom aids like grab bars, shower seat, anti-skid tiles, motion sensor lighting, fall-prevention sensors, floor levelling, availability of balcony and so on.

- **Commercial:** Terms of sale/ lease/ rental, property purchase/ rental cost, monthly maintenance costs and the inclusions and exclusions in these monthly charges. Usually housekeeping, usage of common facilities, engagement programmes, access to medical services as well as concierge services are included in the monthly charges. Medicines, groceries and other incidentals are not included. Food charges may be additional as it's an optional expense.

- **Security and safety measures:** CCTV cameras, grills in the balcony, windows, visitor monitoring systems, door cameras, veracity of security staff and so forth.

- **Heath and medical facilities:** Availability of medical facilities and resident doctor/ nurse/ physiotherapist, tie-ups with a leading hospital, frequency of check-ups, on-site ambulance, emergency response systems and procedures, readiness of the place to offer assisted living facilities in case one needs nursing or full-time care, protocol in place in case of sudden demise of a resident.

- **Food:** Vegetarian or non-vegetarian, cuisines and variety offered, frequency and schedule of meals, customization of meal plans in case of special dietary requirements, nutritionist on board, restrictions on cooking at home, rules around liquor, hygiene of the dining hall and staff and so on.

- **Staff:** Staff-to-resident ratio, staff training and experience, staff on duty overnight, etc.

- **Common facilities:** Type of recreational facilities available and their age-friendliness, engagement programmes and their diversity, power back-up of common areas, cleaning and maintenance of common areas.

- **Developer/Builder profile:** Reputation and experience of the developer, their involvement in operations post hand-over.

There are some common questions that are put to us by older adults who are considering senior living options. The responses shared here are valid for most senior living communities around India but do check specifically for the project you are considering.

1. **What is the benefit of staying in a senior living community vis-á-vis at home?**
   A senior living community offers holistic care while taking care of your day-to-day needs like cooking, housekeeping, medical care and also social engagement.

It's all available under one roof in a safe, secure and supported environment with age-friendly amenities.

2. **Will a senior living community take care of me as my needs change with age?**
   There are four different formats of senior living—active or independent living, assisted living, nursing care and hospice care. Communities that can adapt to your evolving needs are called Continuing Care Retirement Communities (CCRC). You must understand this about the project during your evaluation process. Refer to the explanation of nine senior-care formats as defined in the CII report on the senior-care sector, included later in this chapter.

3. **Are senior living communities only for seniors? Will my family be allowed to visit and stay with me?**
   A senior living community is like any other residential community. It's your home and your family members and guests are welcome to your home and can stay with you.

4. **Is there an entry age to stay in a senior living home?**
   You can buy a senior living home at any age but you can move in once you are above fifty-five.

5. **Can I sell my home in a senior living community?**
   Like any other home you own, you can decide what you want to do with it.

6. **Can I stay in a senior living community for a short term before I decide to move in for the long term?**
Many operational communities used to offer trial stay in pre-pandemic times but they are on halt currently. However, you can still do a site visit and get a better idea of what's on offer. You can also rent a home for a short term before you make a decision to move in bag and baggage.

What would be the right age to move into a senior living community, we wonder? Seniors themselves seem to prefer to move during their later years when they feel the need for extra help and support. Kunjur is in her sixties and feels she still has a few years before she will be ready to take the plunge. However, both Mohit Nirula, CEO Columbia Pacific Communities, and Adarsh Narahari, CEO of Primus Lifespaces, concur in their opinion that 'earlier the better'. The argument being that it allows a person to find their tribe of friends, settle down better and find the support that they may need in case of difficult situations. We find Neel and Devangi sharing a similar concern about their mother Urmila. They feel at her age it would be challenging for her to find like-minded people and adjust to a new environment. However, Raiker, who is in her seventies seems to have faced no such issues and neither have her co-residents at Primus Reflection—Anjali Kulkarni or Chandrashekhar, whom we met to understand more about their life in a senior living community. They all have similar stories to tell of relaxed living, surrounded by friends and supported by a caring staff. So, the right time to move may come down to personal choice.

However, is moving to a senior living community a straightforward decision for all? Is it a financially viable option for every senior?

Rajit Mehta, MD & CEO, Antara Senior Care, clarifies that it's a misnomer that a senior living is not a viable option. 'If you were living in a condominium, you will be paying a monthly maintenance fee of Rs 3–4 per sq ft that covers maintenance of common areas which doesn't cover maintenance inside your home or access to healthcare services. At best it may include access to a club and common amenities. However, if you were living in a senior living community, you would be paying Rs 6–6.5 per sq ft which covers common area maintenance, access to healthcare services, engagement activities, access to common amenities, housekeeping, concierge services and so on. So going by this, it's not expensive at all.'

Adarsh Narahari, CEO of Primus Lifespaces, chimes in saying, 'We are good at calculating direct costs and not indirect costs. At a retirement community we have economies of scale as the same staff is serving multiple households so the cost of serving is cheaper than serving a single household. Indirect costs when accounted for escalate the total cost many times over. If you were to include expenses like travelling to run errands or for doctor visits, entertainment opportunities, etc., your monthly expenses turn out to be much higher vis-a-vis your monthly maintenance fee at a senior living community.' The table below gives an overview of typical monthly expenses for an older couple. In comparison to this, the monthly maintenance fee for a couple staying at Primus Reflection is about Rs 25,000 per month, which is inclusive of food, engagement, common amenities usage, housekeeping, basic healthcare and concierge services.

Sl No.	Expense Item	Amount (Rs)
1	Food (including snacks): Rs 250 per day per person	15,000
2	Utilities (electricity and water bills): with air conditioner	5,000
3	Maid salary with consumables (for cleaning)	4,000
4	Cook's salary	3,000
5	Common area maintenance charges	6,000
6	Doctor consultation expense	2,000
7	Entertainment expenses (eating out, movies, plays etc.)	2,000
8	Fuel costs	3,000
9	Internet and DTH TV	2,500
10	Gym and club charges	1,500
11	If self-owned (approx. monthly cost of AMCs and other repairs such as waterproofing, repainting etc.)	3,000
12	Routine repairs and maintenance (plumber, carpenter etc.)	1,500
	TOTAL MONTHLY EXPENSE	**48,500**

Source: Primus Lifespaces Pvt. Ltd.

But, how about those who would like to continue living in their own homes for various reasons? Is there a way to meet your evolving requirements without having to uproot you from your current home?

Megha Jindal lives in Thailand with her husband and kids while her brother is settled in the US. Her parents continue to live by themselves in Delhi. She is conscious of her parents' changing needs and realizes that sooner or later few difficult discussions will be necessary and choices will have to be made, irrespective of whether everyone in the family likes it or not. She doesn't see her parents agreeing to moving into a senior living community as they are accustomed to their neighbourhood. As many experts will tell you, it's highly inadvisable to force an elder out of their comfort zone unless they are willingly ready to make that move, as it can add to confusion and stress. Relocating with either of the kids is not an option for the parents, for reasons discussed earlier. So, what options does Jindal and her family have? You may have faced a similar situation yourself, as an older adult or an offspring and wondered what the solution could be. Here are some things Jindal has identified as her next steps:

- Parents go on living on their own until both are relatively healthy and able to manage their daily life, given that this is their personal preference and should be accepted and respected.
- Step up support through part-time/ full-time help.
- Facilitate incremental improvements that improve their life quality—for instance, enable ongoing engagement opportunities via senior community

groups like Silver Talkies, organize small group trips, two-to three-week health retreats, find ways to improve their dwelling to support their ageing needs.

- In case of a big medical episode that changes their independence, identify concrete options to continue in their own home with enhanced professional support or parents move in with either child or create a co-housing arrangement with one or more of her mother's sisters as she is very close to them.

What Jindal is thinking of is the concept of aging in place. Aging in place is a term used to describe a person living in the residence of their choice, for as long as they are able to, as they age. What this essentially entails is that you put a plan in place today to age comfortably in your current home tomorrow, while maintaining or even improving your health and independence. It involves making suitable and necessary changes at the residence to make it age friendly and also identifying and including a support framework that can be mobilized when needed. Some of the areas of planning include finances, home improvement, healthcare support, social and emotional engagement, emergency response system, safety and security, and other support services.

A major requirement for enabling ageing in place is to 'elderize' a home as Saumyajit Roy, CEO and co-founder Emoha Eldercare calls it. A recent article 'Aging-in-Place

Strategy for the Next Generation'[4] by BCG highlights that the trend of aging in place is gaining popularity and credibility around the world. With certain adaptations, the experiences and outcomes are as good as or even better than, those of residents in assisted-living facilities or nursing homes. The costs are lower too. Aging in place offers blended care, in which formal staff is mixed with informal labour—the largely unpaid caretaking and housekeeping provided by family, friends, and elderly people themselves.

Elderizing a home entails a careful assessment of the living conditions, taking control of avoidable factors and fall-proofing the house by making any necessary changes architecturally or otherwise.

Sunita Thakker lives in Mumbai with her husband. A few months ago, while on a weekend stay at their holiday home, Thakker had a fall in the bathroom due to a wet floor. Unable to get herself up, she kept calling out to her staff for help but to no avail. With no support available she somehow dragged herself to the basin and got up using the basin for support. This agonizing incident shook her up forcing her to make amends and make changes both in her Mumbai and weekend home—across different areas like bathroom, kitchen, staircase, entrance, etc. She now wears a remote bell around her neck in the night when she is alone so that her staff can be alerted in their quarters in case a similar situation were to arise again. She has put up a board with emergency numbers for ambulances, hospitals, doctors at all levels of the house. She is in the process of installing an elevator at her weekend home and also has a wheelchair on standby.

Anup Misra and his wife took it upon themselves to elderize homes of both sets of parents in Gurugram and Goa. Multiple health conditions faced by his mother made it increasingly difficult for her to come down from the first floor of their two-storied home in Gurugram. A fall a few months ago led her to completely lose confidence in walking independently and she continues to walk with the support of a walker. Moving his mother to the ground-floor bedroom and converting a study into a bedroom for his father while retrofitting both their bathrooms has eased life for everyone in the house. Misra's father-in-law in Goa has been losing motor control over the last couple of years, making it very difficult for them to continue to stay in their large home. The family decided to sell off their big house and move the couple into a smaller and more manageable home. Both homes are now adapted to accommodate movement of a wheelchair, whenever needed. Bathrooms and the kitchen have been modified to make them age friendly. Misra's mother's room has alarm bells strategically located in three different areas to help her alert others in case of a fall. Her bedroom has a bed suited to her height and other custom-made furniture to suit her needs. Many other similar changes have been done in the two homes to avoid any mishaps and keep the elders safe and secure.

Why is elderizing a home so important? Dr Arvind Kasthuri, Chief of Medical Services, St John's Medical College Hospital, Bengaluru, tells us that falls are a very common issue among older adults and the incidence of falls increases as one ages. The World Health Organization estimates that 28 to 35 per cent of older adults experience a fall each year which is equivalent to one in three people.[5] Many falls result in minor injuries only but some can be serious—causing fractures, disability and resulting in a debilitating effect on health requiring long-term care and rehabilitation.[6] Dr Kasthuri says that many factors contribute to why older persons are prone to falls. Some of these factors may be age related—visual problems, hearing impairment, weakness of the muscles, arthritis, difficulty in walking or balance control, among others. Other factors could be extrinsic and avoidable, such as a slippery floor, loose rugs or carpets, clutter on the floors, poor lighting or non-usage of a walking stick or walker when advisable. In addition to these, there can be other contributing factors like side effects of medicines, dizziness due to sudden drop in blood pressure or neurological ailments like Parkinson's or Alzheimer's disease. A third of falls can be prevented, says Dr Kasthuri. While some homes may require certain architectural changes, many of these issues can be addressed by incorporating simple modifications.

Here are some home improvement ideas that can reduce the risk of falls.

Bathrooms

Bathrooms are the highest-risk category area where most falls happen. You can reduce the risk category of this area by introducing some of the following suggested measures.

- Install anti-skid tiles on the floor or give your tiles an anti-skid coating.
- Install grab bars at key areas especially next to shower area, wash basin and the toilet area.
- Install raised toilet seats for ease of use.
- Install a shower seat especially if you have blood pressure or vertigo issues or if you cannot stand for too long.
- Use an anti-slip shower mat in the bathroom.
- Install mixer taps to avoid any scalding accidents with hot water.
- Replace overhead or rain showers with hand showers as they are easier to use.
- Ensure the bathroom is well lit so that you can spot the wet floor. Dry up wet bathrooms immediately.
- Make your shelves accessible and place them at comfortable height so that you don't have to either overreach or bend down to take things.
- Replace bathroom locks with locks that are easy to operate and can be unlocked from outside if needed.

Across the House

- Be careful around the threshold and steps. Slippery or uneven/cobbled floors are hazardous. Remodel these to make them safe.

- Add lift or ramps to the house where needed or possible, in place of staircases.
- Install handrails on the staircases or important areas of the house.
- Install anti-skid strips on stairs or ramps.
- Ensure there is good lighting across the house, especially for staircases, pathways, kitchen and bathroom. Sharp lights are avoidable as they are not elder-friendly. Install motion-sensor lights to avoid any falls during the night.
- Ensure your bed and chairs are at a comfortable height.
- Avoid furniture that is non-sturdy, has wheels or sharp edges.
- Install bed rails to provide extra support when getting on or off the bed.
- Declutter and make the floor areas clutter free, taking away any objects that may cause a fall including wires, furniture and even pets.
- Remove loose rugs or carpets.
- Wear good, anti-skid footwear.
- Make shelves accessible in the kitchen and wardrobes.
- Install fall sensors that can alert a loved one of a fall.
- Install smoke detectors in the house.
- Leverage technology like Alexa devices to create emergency response systems such that you can easily reach your loved one in case of an unfortunate incident.

- Install adequate and easy-to-use security devices to ensure your safety like smart video doorbells, CCTV cameras, panic alarm systems, and so on.

The above list is only indicative to give you an idea of the changes that can be brought about in your existing home so that you can continue to live there comfortably without any fear or worry. Roy tells us that there are about 125 interventions possible within a home at an investment of about Rs 2–2.5 lakhs to completely elderize a house. He emphasizes the need for a qualified architect to assess your house, suggest and carry out all the necessary changes.

In addition to home improvement, the other major component is healthcare support. As one ages, a natural decline in physical abilities can be expected but keeping a keen eye on your health and lifestyle could add life to your years rather than the other way round. Keeping an active physical and mental-health routine, enabling social and emotional engagement by joining groups of like-minded individuals can enhance your well-being and keep loneliness and isolation at bay. For health-related support, you can explore options like healthcare at home that give you access to services like trained attendant or a nurse for caregiving needs, a doctor on call, medical equipment for hire, physiotherapy, dental services, diagnostic services etc. In today's times, adapting to technology and picking up necessary skills can help you leverage facilities like teleconsultation when a physical doctor visit may not be needed. With online shopping options mushrooming by the minute, you could take care of your grocery lists or medicine orders through mobile apps and websites and create much more time in your schedules to do activities of your interest. Technology can also come in handy in the form of wearables like GPS tracker, health vital monitors, fitness trackers and so on that can help you and your loved ones keep a close eye on your health parameters. You can also apply some old-school measures for handling emergencies.

- Enlist support of friendly and trustworthy neighbours and have their contact numbers handy.
- Leave a spare key with a trusted neighbour or friend for easy accessibility in case of emergency.
- Place a list of important contact numbers at a visible location like on the fridge door, almirah or any other regularly accessed surface. These numbers could be of the older adult's doctor, preferred hospital and family members to be notified in case of an emergency. The list should also include other important information such as blood group, usual medication, allergies if any, among others.
- Keep select near and dear ones informed of the medical history and insurance records.

According to the CII Senior Care Industry Report India of 2018 there are nine senior-care formats that are relevant in India. There are various options available for you to choose from based on your health condition and situation.

Format	Description
Independent Living Community	Apartment complexes, condominiums, cooperatives and other such retirement communities, offering private residences designed for the independent senior. These types of communities do not provide medical services but instead provide seniors with hassle-free living, with some recreational facilities. A seniors-only housing community could be a stand-alone facility or a part of a larger housing project as an area, tower or cluster of apartments/homes.
Assisted Living Community	Assisted living offers help with non-medical aspects of daily activities in an atmosphere of separate, private living units. It can be likened to congregate living for residents less able to function independently in all aspects of their daily lives.
Skilled Nursing Facility	Skilled nursing facilities offer the most intensive level of care on the residential care continuum. Skilled nursing facilities are equipped to handle individuals with 24-hour nursing needs, post-operative recuperation, or complex medical-care demands, as well as chronically-ill individuals who can no longer live independently. Such facilities may be free-standing or part of a senior community. SNFs may specialize in short-term or acute nursing care, intermediate or long-term skilled nursing care.
Continuing Care Retirement Community (CCRC)	A Continuing Care Retirement Community (CCRC) offers seniors a facility that combines housing, services and health care, allowing seniors to enjoy a private residential lifestyle with the opportunity of independence and the assurances of long-term health care. Within the CCRC, there are three types of care available, providing a phased approach to elderly living accommodations: independent living, in which the person lives on their own in an apartment or cottage-style housing; assisted-living offering some level of assistance for residents; and/or skilled nursing care, for residents whose health is deteriorating

Format	Description
Memory Care Facility	Memory-care facilities provide increased levels of care and safety for individuals with Alzheimer's and dementia.
Senior Day Care facility	Day-care centers provide stimulation and rehabilitation to elders providing medical care and related procedures.
Home Care	Services provided to seniors within the senior's home, addressing clinical and non-clinical support needs including engagement activities, ADL assistance support, housekeeping, home engineering support, nutrition support.
PWD Care	These are for senior citizens with special children who may have autism, cerebral palsy, Down's Syndrome or are spastics. The model takes care of such senior citizens with special children living in the Senior Care Centre, and after the demise of the parents, cares for the special children until their death
Palliative Care	Palliative care is a multidisciplinary approach to specialized medical and nursing care for people with life-limiting illnesses. It focuses on providing people with relief from the symptoms, pain, physical stress and mental stress of the terminal diagnosis.

Source: *CII Senior Care Industry Report India 2018*

Ageing at home or beyond is a choice that you can make for yourself based on your preferences and needs. Yes, there are many factors like unmet finances or lack of insurance coverage which make these choices difficult and unrealistic for some, but you need not wait for a medical episode or loneliness to set in to start considering your options. In India, availability of professionally managed senior living communities, quality and skilled home healthcare services and technologically advanced solutions is still far from satisfactory, however the scenario is fast changing and improving. You could empower yourself with an understanding of the landscape of options available and evaluate them, choosing what feels right for you. It may take some conditioning to accept the idea of ageing beyond home but be willing to make some trade-offs and look beyond typical social norms to make a choice that will be best suited for you in the long run. Some discussions while difficult need to be had as Jindal has realized, 'We don't talk about it. Each caught up in their own life and it's a sensitive subject with no clear or easy answers. I tend to be more logical and my brother more emotional which makes these conversations tricky. He gets super anxious and guilt-ridden even thinking about these situations. I feel the bigger challenge is helping parents take active agency in their old-age, facilitating to the best extent possible the life they would like to live.'

As you have read in the previous chapters, age need not be debilitating, despite unavoidable physical changes. This is the reason adaptability tools and measures exist. *Leading a life of dignity is what we all deserve. Make it yours.*

Acknowledgements

It takes a village to write a book. We would have never had that appreciation had we not embarked on this journey that has been as enriching as exacting. Here's to that village—

Shiny Das, who found our website Silver Talkies, liked our work and saw the idea of a book there. Shreya Punj, our wonderful editor, whose words were comfort and confidence when we wondered about being on the right track. To Rea Mukherjee and Aparna Abhijit for taking the story forward.

To Akila Krishnakumar, for being our mentor and a believer in the Silver Talkies journey.

To Shiv Kumar, our member and legal expert who has always been around to help navigate the legal jargon and much more.

To Kala Sunder, for always having us in her thoughts.

To our spouses, Pankaj and Manoj, and our children, Akshat, Vanya and Aahan, for their support and understanding, when it was needed.

Our parents have been the first inspiration for Silver Talkies, which led to this. Thanking them will never be enough.

To Chitra Nair, an invaluable part of our all-women team at Silver Talkies.

To Paul Singh and our 1Gen team for being the catalyst.

This book quotes several experts from various eldercare services and health-related fields. We have had the privilege of associating with many of them over the years and were honoured to make new connections as we went in search of guidance. We thank all of them for their trust in our work and the generosity of their time, despite their busy schedules through the pandemic.

Writing can be a lonely activity. We started working on this book during the pandemic, which was a tough time for all of us emotionally. We were lucky to have a rock-solid support system of friends and family to fall back on who believed we could write a book, offered us encouragement, cheered us on and were always around to share doubts, drafts, and (more than the occasional) whine with. They say friendships hold you up. They truly do. Across many corners of life. To Anupama Rajagopalan, Aseem Sood, Gail Sinha, Gaurav Garg, Hamida Parkar, Kuhu Jain, Kazim Parkar, K.V. Jitesh, Mahesh Kumar, Manjula Ramaswamy, Natesh Shetty, Nihar Shah, Pavan Voruganti, Paromita, Preety Banerjee, Rohin Govindrajan Sheetal Mehta, Shobha Naresh, Saurav Chakraborty, Sumit Chauhan, Sreemoyee Chatterjee, V. Shrinath and Veenu Misra for being there.

Always. P.S. Bhawana and Sejal Mehta for sharing the ride. Thank you.

Aarti David, Kushalrani Gulab, Ruchira Chaudhary and Usha Rajagopalan, our first guides, helped us understand all about proposals and chapter structures. Nithya Shanti for opening new doorways of clarity and mindfulness.

To every senior citizen we spoke to for this book; everyone who gave us time and shared their thoughts— Thank you for the conversations, the insight and the mirror you looked into honestly to tell us how it is. We may not have been able to incorporate everyone in these pages but each and every interaction has been a source of deeper understanding and invaluable insight into ageing and how it is being navigated by urban older adults in India. A big thank you to all the children who reached out with their parents' stories and shared their highs and lows with us—not always an easy thing to do.

A book that is interview and reportage-based is not possible without the many people making those connections. Gratitude to all those who helped us with reach outs.

To all the volunteers, champions, experts, supporters and patrons who have been our cheerleaders consistently. You know who you are.

And last but never in the least, to our in-house sources of positive energy—the members of Silver Talkies Club, whose interactions, spirit, kindness and innovative ideas remain our constant learning, inspiration, wonder and motivation to stay the course.

Resource Guide

Older adults in India and their families often feel there is a lack of easily available resources and information of services, activities and tools that could be useful for them. This resource guide is far from comprehensive but is meant to be a start and therefore often links to portals that are updated on a continuous basis to reflect defunct services and changed numbers. This guide is also based on expert suggestions and recommendations we have come across while working on this book and over many years of work with older adults for Silver Talkies. You can connect with us on connect@silvertalkies.com to help you find more opportunities specific to your city.

Chapter 1: Older & Bolder: Changing Face of Age in India

1. Elders' Helplines
    Nightingales and the Bengaluru City Police: 1090 /
    080-22943226

Kolkata Police: 98300 88884
Elder Line, Mumbai Police: 1090
Helpage India, Chennai: 1800 180 1253
Police helpline, Chennai: 1253
Pune: 1090

2. Modern Elder Academy: https://www.modernelder
   academy.com/
3. Silver Talkies: www.silvertalkies.com; 6362890768
4. Recommended reading on Maintenance and Welfare
   of Parents and Senior Citizens Act 2007: https://c1.
   silvertalkies.com/care/description?id=450

Chapter 2: Keeping Pace: Why Movement Matters With Age

1. Activity Heals: badrirao@activityheals.com
2. Growing Young, an online fitness programme for
   seniors by physiotherapists: https://growingyoung.
   co.in/
3. Dr Poonam Bajaj: Poonam.Bajaj@rfhospital.org
4. Devika Mehta Kadam, Dance Movement Therapy:
   https://synchronyindia.com/index.php
5. Yoga classes for senior citizens: https://c1.silvertalkies.
   com/care/event_detail?id=59
6. Sujata Cowlagi: http://www.pragyayoga.com/
7. Qigong, Tai Chi: Kadihai Martial Arts, Mysore http://
   kadihai.com/
8. Vital Force Taichi Academy, Bengaluru: 9449633267
9. Tai Chi, Mumbai: https://www.sifucarltonhill.com/

10. Dance movement therapy for Parkinson's disease: https://www.parkinsonssocietyindia.com/

Chapter 3: The Mind Map: Learn to Be Kind to Your Mind

1. Dr Santosh Bangar's Mind Clinic: https://icare4 seniors.in/
2. Tanvi Mallya: http://tanvimallyaseldercare.in/
3. The National Institute of Mental Health & Neuro Sciences (NIMHANS): https://nimhans.ac.in/
4. Nightingales Medical Trust: https://www. nightingaleseldercare.com/index.html
5. Alzheimer's and Related Disorders Society of India (ARDSI): https://ardsi.org/
6. Echoing Healthy Ageing: https://www.echoing healthyageing.com/
7. For information on dementia care, support groups for caregivers and other useful resources across cities: https://dementiacarenotes.in/
8. Agewell Foundation: https://www.agewellfoundation. org/

Chapter 4: The Spirit Within: How Spirituality Can Help

1. Maitreyi Dadashreeji: https://www.maitribodh.org/
2. Arun Wakhlu: https://pragatileadership.com/
3. Nithya Shanti: http://www.nithyashanti.com/

4. Brahmaviharas: https://www.britannica.com/topic/brahmavihara
5. Byron Katie: https://thework.com/
6. Tom Verghese: https://culturalsynergies.com/
7. Chardi Kala: http://sikhlens.com/pdf/PDV%20Chardikala.pdf
8. Dr Sujata Shetty: https://penguin.co.in/book/99-not-out/

Chapter 5: Master a Second Innings: Adding Life to Your Years

1. Tata Institute of Social Sciences, Nirantar Continuing Education Program: https://admissions.tiss.edu/admissions/stp/programmes/
2. Shoolini University: https://shooliniuniversity.com/
3. Unfold Consulting: https://unfold-consulting.com/
4. Nightingales' Jobs 60+: https://www.nightingaleseldercare.com/jobs60plus.html
5. Hum Communities: https://www.humcommunities.in/
6. Senior Able Citizens Reemployment in Dignity: https://sacred.dosje.gov.in/index.php

Chapter 6: All We Need Is Love: Why Companionship Matters

1. Happy Seniors: Madhav Damle: 80071 93397; happyseniors19@gmail.com
2. Thikana Shimla: 93308 43394; thikana_shimla@yahoo.co.in

3. Thodu Needa: Contact N.M. Rajeshwari on thoduneeda2010@gmail.com or visit their FB page: https://www.facebook.com/thoduneeda.sewa; You may also call: 8106367014

4. Vina Mulya Amulya Sewa (VMAS), Ahmedabad, and across India. Contact Natubhai Patel on natubhai.vmas@gmail.com

5. Just Older Youth (JOY): https://www.facebook.com/groups/129844620448652

Chapter 7: Social Networks: The Wellness Secret Sauce

1. Silver Talkies Club: 6362890768; connect@silvertalkies.com

2. Dignity Foundation: https://dignityfoundation.com; 6138 1100

3. Nightingales Elders Enrichment Centre: 080 2334 2929

4. Humjoli: https://www.facebook.com/jalvayusector21park/?ref=page_internal; 98996 72403

5. Laughter Yoga: https://laughteryoga.org/

6. Maya Care Foundation: http://www.mayacare.org/

7. Blue Zones: https://www.bluezones.com/

Chapter 8: Ageing at Home and Beyond: Getting Ready

1. For a comprehensive guide to retirement homes and assisted living facilities across India, read: https://

c1.silvertalkies.com/care/magazine/March-2019/ Retirement_Communities_in_North_West_and_ East_India

2. Association of Senior Living India: http://www.asli. org.in/

3. The 2018 Senior Care Industry Report by CII lists several services in eldercare and senior living categories. It can be downloaded here: https://www.cii.in/ PublicationDetail.aspx?enc=M1jmdd7m0jZwhCrdz/ WMqbntPNvfl/+RqYOANxC7X2U=

4. https://emoha.com/

5. http://primuslife.in/

6. https://www.columbiacommunities.in/

Notes

Introduction

1   PTI, 'Elderly people worried about maintaining social life: Survey', *The Times of India*, October 6, 2018. https://timesofindia.indiatimes.com/india/elderly-people-worried-about-maintaining-social-life-survey/articleshow/66097077.cms

Chapter 1: Older & Bolder: Changing Face of Age in India

1   Carl Honoré, *Bolder: How to Age Better and Feel Better About Ageing* (Knopf, Canada, 2019), p. 12
2   Arnsberg, a West German town, started a Department of Future Aging (DFA) in 2004 for its older residents. The DFA supports projects and resources that empower and enable senior citizens to remain an active part of the community.

Priti Salian, 'Is This the World's Most Aging-Friendly City?', *Reasons To Be Cheerful*, May 18, 2021 https://reasonstobecheerful.world/is-this-the-worlds-most-aging-friendly-city/

3   Shubhra Dixit, 'Death Wish', *The Caravan*, May 31, 2020
    Superscript: In 2018, Mumbai couple Narayan and Irawati Lavate, then in their late 70s and 80s, petitioned the Supreme Court of India for the right to die together with dignity. The Lavates do not have children and sought permission for physician assisted suicide before they became bedridden and dependant on others for their care. Active euthanasia, what the Lavates petitioned for is administering lethal compounds to end life and is illegal in India. Passive euthanasia in now permissible since 2018 but the patient must be either terminally ill or in a vegetative state to be considered a candidate. Since the Lavates do not fall under this category their petition has not been accepted.

4   Phalasha Nagpal, 'The Hidden Paradoxes In India's Latest Life Expectancy Figures', *The Wire*, August 14, 2020. https://science.thewire.in/health/india-life-expectancy-birth-srs-2013-2017-gender/

5   PTI, '60% senior want to work post retirement, spend on leisure travel: Survey', *Business Standard*, January 14, 2021. https://www.business-standard.com/article/current-affairs/60-seniors-want-to-

work-post-retirement-spend-on-leisure-travel-survey-121011401344_1.html

6 'The Greysians of IG That Will Inspire You To Embrace Your Natural Hair', *Her World*, May 12, 2021

7 National Crime Records Bureau, *Crime in India, Statistics Volume-I*, (2019), https://ncrb.gov.in/sites/default/files/CII%202019%20Volume%201.pdf Staff Reporter, 'Capital accounts for most crimes against senior citizens' *The Pioneer*, September 17, 2021. https://www.dailypioneer.com/2021/state-editions/capital-accounts-for-most-crimes-against-senior-citizens--ncrb.html

Chapter 2: Keeping Pace: Why Movement Matters With Age

1 Jayashree Narayanan, 'Meet Tripat Singh, the 75-year-old vegan who is an inspiration to Virat, Anushka', *Indian Express*, October 13, 2020. https://indianexpress.com/article/lifestyle/fitness/tripat-singh-fitness-vegan-diet-plant-protein-sources-virat-kohli-anushka-sharma-instagram-6561519/

2 Jovita Aranha, 'He Battled Epilepsy at 62. 23 Years Later, He Is 86 and Has Cycled 4,00,000 Kms', *The Better India*, February 15, 2019. https://www.thebetterindia.com/172555/bengaluru-railway-retired-cycling-trekking-running/

3   Ria Das, 'Usha Soman Becomes The Oldest Woman To Complete Sandakphu Trek', *She The People*, February 20, 2021. https://www.shethepeople.tv/film-theatre/usha-soman-oldest-woman-complete-sandakphu-trek/

4   Lin TW, Tsai SF, Kuo YM. 'Physical Exercise Enhances Neuroplasticity and Delays Alzheimer's Disease'. *US National Library of Medicine, PMC*, vol 4 (December 12, 2018), https://www.ncbi.nlm.nih.gov/pmc/articles/PMC6296269/

5   Pitchai P, Dedhia HB, Bhandari N, Krishnan D, D'Souza NR, Bellara JM. 'Prevalence, risk factors, circumstances for falls and level of functional independence among geriatric population: A descriptive study.' *Indian Journal of Public Health*, Vol 63, (March 12, 2019), https://www.ijph.in/article.asp?issn=0019-557X;year=2019;volume=63;issue=1;spage=21;epage=26;aulast=Pitchai

6   Chandrika Radhakrishnan, Dancing Away The Years, *Silver Talkies*, February 19, 2019. https://c1.silvertalkies.com/care/magazine/February-2019/Dancing_Away_The_Years

7   Schuch FB, Dunn AL, Kanitz AC, Delevatti RS, Fleck MP. 'Moderators of response in exercise treatment for depression: A systematic review'. *Journal of Affective Disorders*, (May, 2016), https://pubmed.ncbi.nlm.nih.gov/26854964/

8   Nerys Williams, The Borg Rating of Perceived Exertion (RPE) scale, *Occupational Medicine*, Volume

67, Issue 5, (July 15, 2017), https://doi.org/10.1093/occmed/kqx063

Chapter 3: The Mind Map: Learn to Be Kind to Your Mind

1 Liaison psychiatrists specialize in the diagnosis and management of psychiatric disorders that are comorbid with general medical and surgical illness.

2 DTE Staff, 'Health ministry survey flags depression symptoms in every third senior citizen in India', *Down To Earth*, January 6, 2021. https://www.downtoearth.org.in/news/health/health-ministry-survey-flags-depression-symptoms-in-every-third-senior-citizen-in-india-74938

3 National Institute of Mental Health and Neuro Sciences, Bengaluru, National Mental Health Survey of India, 2015–16, Prevalence, Pattern and Outcomes, (2016), http://indianmhs.nimhans.ac.in/Docs/Report2.pdf

4 The treatment gap refers to the difference that exists between the number of people who need mental health care and those who receive care. It's a World Health Organization concept.

5 Akhil Kadidal, 'IISc's Alzheimer's study goes mobile', *Deccan Herald*, Bengaluru, March 1, 2020. https://www.deccanherald.com/city/bengaluru-infrastructure/iiscs-alzheimers-study-goes-mobile-809398.html

6 Swapna Kishore, Indian movies depicting dementia, *Dementia Care Notes* (July 2020), https://

dementiacarenotes.in/resources/indian-movies-depicting-dementia/

7 https://whichmeamitoday.wordpress.com/
8 https://dementiacarenotes.in/
9 https://egazette.nic.in/WriteReadData/2017/175248.pdf
10 Hector Garcia and Francesc Miralles, *Ikigai: The Japanese Secret To A Long And Happy Life* (Penguin Random House UK, 2017)
11 Reshmi Chakraborty, 'Why This 'Tuition Uncle' Should Be An Example For Senior Citizens Wishing To Volunteer', *Silver Talkies*, December 4, 2017. https://c1.silvertalkies.com/care/magazine/December-2017/Why_This_Tuition_Uncle_Should_Be_An_Example_For_Senior_Citizens_Wishing_To_Volunteer
12 Matt Walker, Sleep is your superpower, *Ted.com*, April 2019. https://www.ted.com/talks/matt_walker_sleep_is_your_superpower

Chapter 4: The Spirit Within: How Spirituality Can Help

1 https://www.maitribodh.org/
2 Wholesome leadership is about framing a clear-cut roadmap and executing actions through self-awareness, people awareness and surrounding awareness. https://pragatileadership.com/blog/wholesome-leadership-an-overview
3 http://www.nithyashanti.com

4 The Brahma Kumaris or Daughters of Brahma movement was founded by Lekhraj Kripalani in the 1930s. The organisation is known for the prominent role that women play in the movement, Sister Shivani being one of them.

5 Louis Hay, *You Can Heal Your Life*. (Hay House UK 2004)

6 Murthy, RSrinivasa & Banerjee, Debanjan. 'Loneliness in Older People: From Analysis to Action'. *World Social Psychiatry*, Vol 3. (August 31, 2021), https://www.worldsocpsychiatry.org/article.asp?issn=2667-1077;year=2021;volume=3;issue=2;spage=120;epage=122;aulast=Murthy

7 Sujata Kelkar Shetty, *99 Not Out!*, (Penguin Random House, 2019)

8 www.shekharkapur.com

Chapter 5: Master a Second Innings: Adding Life to Your Years

1 https://www.icaa.cc/activeagingandwellness/wellness.htm

2 Sarah Bahr, 'Yuh-Jung Youn becomes the first Korean woman in Oscar history to win best supporting actress', *New York Times*, April 25, 2021. https://www.nytimes.com/2021/04/25/movies/yuh-jung-youn-minari-oscars-win.html

3 Michael Sullivan, 'Meet The 74-Year-Old Queen Of Bangkok Street Food Who Netted

A Michelin Star', *The Salt, NPR,* June 26, 2019. https://www.npr.org/sections/thesalt/2019/06/26/732529154/meet-the-74-year-old-queen-of-bangkok-street-food-who-netted-a-michelin-star

4 'KBC helped change my world, says an emotional Amitabh in new promo', *The Tribune,* December 3, 2021. https://www.tribuneindia.com/news/entertainment/kbc-helped-change-my-world-says-an-emotional-amitabh-in-new-promo-345940

5 Zaria Gorvett, 'How elders can reinvigorate the workforce', *BBC, Worklife,* November 15, 2019. https://www.bbc.com/worklife/article/20191112-how-the-elderly-can-reinvigorate-the-workforce

6 Reshmi Chakraborty, 'Senior citizens put themselves back in job market, employers should focus on this growing social need', *Firstpost,* June 12, 2017. https://www.firstpost.com/business/senior-citizens-put-themselves-back-in-job-market-employers-should-focus-on-this-growing-social-need-3550903.html

7 Rebecca Perron, 'The Value of Experience: Age Discrimination Against Older Workers Persists', *AARP* (2018), https://www.aarp.org/content/dam/aarp/research/surveys_statistics/econ/2018/value-of-experience-age-discrimination-highlights.doi.10.26419-2Fres.00177.002.pdf

8 https://www.instagram.com/p/BXGN0-nlwkv/?utm_source=ig_embed&ig_rid=e83c80d5-c295-4695-8f00-ee131dc67299

9 'Government's SACRED senior citizens job portal opens from today', *DNA*, Oct 1, 2021. https://www. dnaindia.com/india/report-government-s-sacred-job-portal-for-senior-citizens-opens-from-today-check-details-sarkari-naukri-jobs-alert-2913606

10 Government of India, Speech of Nirmala Sitharaman, Minister of Finance, Budget 2022-23. https://www. indiabudget.gov.in/doc/budget_speech.pdf

11 http://sacred.dosje.gov.in/index.php

Chapter 6: All We Need Is Love: Why Companionship Matters

1 Eve Pell, The Race Grows Sweeter Near Its Final Lap, *The New York Times, Modern Love*, 24 January 2013. https://www.nytimes.com/2013/01/27/style/modern-love-the-race-grows-sweeter-near-its-final-lap.html

2 Ministry of Health and Family Welfare, Longitudinal Ageing Study in India (LASI), Wave-1, (2020), https://www.iipsindia.ac.in/sites/default/files/LASI_India_Report_2020_compressed.pdf

3 Rema Nagarajan, '15 million elderly Indians live all alone', *The Times of India*, Oct 1, 2014. https:// timesofindia.indiatimes.com/india/15-million-elderly-indians-live-all-alone-census/articleshow/43948392.cms

4 Samanta, T., Varghese, S.S. 'Love in the Time of Aging: Sociological Reflections on Marriage, Gender and Intimacy in India'. *Ageing International* 44, (2019), https://doi.org/10.1007/s12126-018-9332-z

5   Jovita Aranha, 'These Senior 'Singles' are Giving People
    the Most Amazing Retirement Goals', *The Better
    India*, April 28, 2018. https://www.thebetterindia.
    com/139533/senior-singles-retirement/

Chapter 7: Social Networks: The Wellness Secret Sauce

1   Aseanplus News, 'South Korea's poor and lonely
    elderly shake their woes away on the dance floors', *The
    Star*, April 17, 2018. https://www.thestar.com.my/
    news/regional/2018/04/17/daytime-discos-a-respite-
    from-anxiety-south-koreas-poor-and-lonely-elderly-
    shake-their-woes-away-on

2   Atul Gawande, *Being Mortal: Medicine and What
    Matters in the End*, (Penguin India, 2014) Chapter 5,
    A Better Life,

3   Holt-Lunstad J, Smith TB, Layton JB, 'Social
    Relationships and Mortality Risk: A Meta-analytic
    Review', *PLoS Medicine*, July 27, 2010. https://doi.
    org/10.1371/journal.pmed.1000316

4   https://www.outlookindia.com/newsscroll/social-
    life-daily-needs-most-worry-elders-living-alone-
    survey/1392016

5   Eileen M. Crimmins, 'Social hallmarks of aging:
    Suggestions for geroscience research', *Ageing
    Research Reviews*, Volume 63, November 2020.
    https://www.sciencedirect.com/science/article/pii/
    S1568163720302713?via%3Dihub.

Chapter 8: Ageing at Home and Beyond: Getting Ready

1 PTI, '60% seniors want to work post-retirement, spend on leisure travel: Survey', *Business Standard*, January 14, 2021. https://www.business-standard. com/article/current-affairs/60-seniors-want-to-work-post-retirement-spend-on-leisure-travel-survey-121011401344_1.html

2 Nishi Malhotra, Retirement Communities in India: An Idea Whose Time Has Come, Silver Talkies, January 23, 2019. https://c1.silvertalkies.com/care/magazine/January-2019/Retirement_Communities_in_India_An_Idea_Whose_Time_Has_Come

3 The report was released at the 2nd Annual Senior Care Conclave, held on 1 October 2019 in New Delhi. It can be downloaded here: https://www.cii.in/PublicationDetail.aspx?enc=M1jmdd7m0jZwhCrdz/WMqbntPNvfl/+RqYOANxC7X2U=

4 An Aging-in-Place Strategy for the Next Generation, February 23, 2022 https://www.bcg.com/publications/2022/aging-in-place-plan-for-next-generation?linkId=155791874

5 WHO global report on falls prevention in older age, Ageing and Health, Maternal, Newborn, Child & Adolescent Health & Ageing, WHO (March 2008)

6 Claudia Wallis, 'Deadly Falls among the Elderly Are on the Rise', *Scientific American*, October 1, 2021. https://www.scientificamerican.com/article/deadly-falls-among-theelderly-are-on-the-rise/

Index